"I pray that you will study this boc
in your church with the love and pc
redeem church conflict, turning it into an opportunity for growth, worship, and kingdom expansion."

Ken Sande, president of Peacemaker Ministries;
author of *The Peacemaker*

"Church conflict is a shameful thing—it hurts, divides, and besmirches the name of Christ. This volume does more than lament the problem. It digs deeply into the experience of the New Testament church to discover a model of forgiveness and redemption that can help the witness of the church to shine once again. May this book help to spawn a whole generation of Acts 15 churches."

Timothy George, founding dean of Beeson Divinity School
at Samford University; general editor of the
Reformation Commentary on Scripture

"Tara and David's guiding concept of 'responding redemptively' deeply resonates with me in my roles as a biblical counselor, pastor, seminary professor, and church consultant. Their understanding that the Bible doesn't provide a formula for redeeming church conflict but a biblical, relational road map, equally resonates. I'm encouraged and equipped, as I believe you will be, by their practical, scriptural wisdom. The gripping way that Tara and David unfold the Scripture-saturated relational principles of *perspective, discernment, leadership,* and *biblical response* provides a real-life narrative applicable to any church conflict."

Bob Kellemen, executive director of the Biblical Counseling Coalition;
author of *Equipping Counselors for Your Church*

"In *Redeeming Church Conflicts* Tara Barthel and David Edling draw on their extensive experience helping brothers and sisters resolve serious divisions in ways that bring glory to Jesus, the prince of peace. Perhaps even more important than the wisdom they have gained from walking with congregations through conflict are the insights that they draw from God's Word itself and their confidence that a deepening grasp of the gospel of God's grace sets hearts free to seek and grant forgiveness and to find the humility to 'maintain the unity of the Spirit in the bond of peace.' Believers and church leaders should read and take to heart the wisdom offered in *Redeeming Church Conflicts* not only when conflict threatens congregations, but also when peace prevails."

Dennis E. Johnson, professor of practical theology,
Westminster Seminary California

"Conflict is inevitable, and Peacemaker Ministries is prepared to equip you to respond. I am excited about this new resource that specifically applies to dealing with conflict within the local church. Tara Barthel and David Edling do the body of Christ a significant service in *Redeeming Church Conflicts*. As a former pastor, I commend this helpful, practical resource to you. Have your staff and your entire church read this book. It will go a long way in creating a culture of peacemaking in your church."

Tim S. Lane, president of Christian Counseling
& Educational Foundation

"Church conflict often ends with Christ's name slandered, the church split, and members bitter and hopeless. *Redeeming Church Conflicts* is that rare book that proves what it promises by showing how the gospel truly affords the church in conflict means of redeeming the seemingly irredeemable. Taking Acts 15 as both an instructive and informative model for redeeming church conflict, the authors illustrate and reinforce their counsel by many and varied case studies aptly demonstrating how to apply redemptive principles of peacemaking. Combining deep, practical wisdom with an unswerving vision of God's glory, Barthel and Edling call the church and its leaders to cast off sinful pragmatic approaches and redeem conflicts to the glory of God and his gospel."

Alfred Poirier, author of *The Peacemaking Pastor*

"Conflicts within the church strike at the heart of our witness to the world, and yet there are very few rigorously biblical resources available on this topic. Dave Edling and Tara Barthel have seamlessly woven together their unique perspectives and lessons learned from many years of working with conflicted churches. More importantly, this book is soundly biblical from beginning to end, with a practical, gospel-centered approach to disputes within the church—large and small. It should be a required text for every seminary student, and it will certainly be a lifeline for every church leader facing difficult conflict situations."

Glenn Waddell, attorney, certified Christian conciliator;
president of Birmingham Theological Seminary

"I wish I had to wonder why a book like this is even needed. But anyone who has spent much time in a church populated by imperfect humans knows that it is. This book delivers exactly what is needed in church conflict: a wealth of biblical wisdom and professional expertise as well as an unflinching challenge toward self-examination and away from angry entrenchment and graceless condemnation. But best of all it offers a huge dose of hope that what is so hurtful and seems only destructive will be used by God to conform his church to his image for his glory."

Nancy Guthrie, Bible teacher and author of the Seeing Jesus in the Old Testament Bible study series

"With delight I commend this much-needed contribution to the field of church conflict intervention from my church conciliation mentor Dave Edling and his colleague Tara Barthel. More than once Dave's clear model has guided me in helping churches in crisis (e.g., that we need to start with God's perspective on this conflict and that leaders must proactively rise up and lead the congregation with biblical wisdom amid conflict). Few writers so richly blend sound theology with seasoned ministry experience, all in a readable case-wise manual that will aid church leaders on all levels. Thank you, Tara and Dave, for helping us help others."

Robert D. Jones, biblical counseling professor at Southeastern Baptist Theological Seminary; author of *Uprooting Anger* and *Pursuing Peace in All Your Relationships*

"*Redeeming Church Conflicts* is biblical, insightful, and practical—based on wisdom born of faithful service to the Lord and a keen understanding of people. Barthel and Edling present a framework for conflict resolution that honors God and redeems what is often times very destructive. Much personal heartache and wounding in Christian ministry could be avoided if church leaders would follow this hermeneutically sound counsel."

Andrew S. Zeller, president, Sangre de Cristo Seminary; Chaplain (COL) U.S. Army (Ret.)

"Dave Edling and Tara Barthel build on their passion for the gospel, people, and peacemaking to bring believers a practical and insightful guide for responding redemptively in the midst of church conflict. The authors' personal experience, wisdom, and biblical faithfulness make this book a must read for anyone who cries out: 'My church is locked in conflict! What can I do?'"

Judy Dabler, reconciliation specialist,
founder of Live at Peace Ministries.

"Looking around at the modern church landscape, it can sometimes seem like bitter irony that the Bible says the manifold wisdom of God is to be shown through his church (Eph. 3:10)—so many conflicts, so many church splits, so many factions! And yet we serve a God who is rich in mercy and does not give up on us. If you find yourself in the midst of church conflict, this book will be a balm to your soul and revive your confidence in the work of the Holy Spirit among his people. Tara Barthel and David Edling have written a wise and tender reminder that our Lord's redemptive purposes extend even today to the most fractious church bodies. Whether you are an ordained leader or a new church member, *Redeeming Church Conflicts* is a must read. It will give you hope that whatever conflicts you are currently in, or will encounter in the future, can be resolved in a holy and purposeful manner to the praise of God's glory."

Carolyn McCulley, author of *Radical Womanhood*
and *Did I Kiss Marriage Goodbye?*

Redeeming
CHURCH
CONFLICTS

*Turning Crisis into
Compassion and Care*

TARA KLENA BARTHEL
AND DAVID V. EDLING

FOREWORD BY KEN SANDE

BakerBooks

a division of Baker Publishing Group
Grand Rapids, Michigan

Published by Baker Books
a division of Baker Publishing Group
P.O. Box 6287, Grand Rapids, MI 49516-6287
www.bakerbooks.com

Printed in the United States of America

Library of Congress Cataloging-in-Publication Data
Barthel, Tara Klena.
    Redeeming church conflicts : turning crisis into compassion and care / Tara Klena
Barthel and David V. Edling ; foreword by Ken Sande.
        p.   cm.
    Includes bibliographical references and index.
    ISBN 978-0-8010-1428-4 (pbk.)
    1. Church controversies. 2. Conflict management—Religious aspects—Christianity.
3. Church management. I. Edling, David V., 1947– II. Title.
BV652.9.B37 2012
250—dc23   2012000560

This book is designed to provide general information on theology, biblical peacemaking, and various aspects of biblical change. It is not intended to provide pastoral, legal, or other professional advice. Readers are encouraged to seek the counsel and oversight of their local church leaders as well as competent professionals relevant to their life situation.

The stories in this book are based on individuals the authors have met or known in real life, but specific details and personal characteristics have been altered or left out to honor privacy. Any resemblance to a specific real person the reader may know is purely coincidental.

The internet addresses, email addresses, and phone numbers in this book are accurate at the time of publication. They are provided as a resource. Baker Publishing Group does not endorse them or vouch for their content or permanence.

12   13   14   15   16   17   18   7   6   5   4   3   2   1

From Dave

This book is dedicated to my wife, Pat,
and to our children and grandchildren,
who bring us such great joy.

And to Tara, my coauthor,
who took my scattered observations about church conflict
and made sense of them.

From Tara

This book is dedicated to my elder and friend, Gary Friesen—
thank you for forgiving and loving me
as we walked through the excruciatingly
painful fire of conflict in the church.

And also to my husband, Fred, and daughters, Sophia and Ella,
to my coauthor, Dave,
and my elder and his wife, Jeff and Amy Laverman—
thank you for helping me to forgive and to love.

Contents

Foreword

The closer the relationship, the more excruciating the conflict. Nowhere does this principle prove itself so vividly as in a family, whether it's biological or spiritual. Most of us have seen the agonizing pain that accompanies the breakdown of a marriage, especially if it is followed by a divorce. The sense of betrayal, anger, bitterness, and hostility that are spawned by the severing of marital bonds can trigger fierce infighting that poisons hearts and relationships for a lifetime.

The same can be said of conflict in a church. Scripture uses familial terms to describe our spiritual relationships—father and mother, son and daughter, brother and sister. We invest our hearts and souls in these relationships; we sacrifice, we share, we struggle, we rejoice, we worship, we grow, we celebrate, and we mourn—*together*. As we do so, our hearts and lives become deeply intertwined, and we develop high expectations of one another.

By God's grace, most of us can overlook the minor disappointments of those expectations and continue to worship and minister together for many wonderful years. But when frequent, prolonged, or serious disagreements pervade our church families, our expectations of one another can be deeply shaken. Small waves of disappointment can grow into tsunamis of conflict that sweep over an entire congregation, destroying relationships, ministries, and the witness of the gospel.

I have seen this destructive process far too many times. In my own community, one of the most vibrant and evangelistic churches in town became tangled in a prolonged battle over vision and leadership style. Instead of responding redemptively, both sides formed well-organized factions that maneuvered for control for years. That church is now a parking lot. Literally. The congregation was shattered and scattered, the building was leveled, and the entire campus is now asphalt. I grieve every time I drive by it.

This is why I am so excited about this book. Through their work with Peacemaker Ministries, my friends Dave and Tara have served dozens of churches that were teetering on the brink of destruction. Again and again, they have immersed themselves in the conflict and distress of entire congregations, listening to story after story, seeing the pain and anger of others, and gaining the trust of people who had lost all ability to trust.

Having gained a passport into the hearts of individuals and opposing factions, Tara and Dave became channels of God's reconciling grace. They have helped people replace worldly suspicion with a kingdom perspective. They have facilitated discernment and understanding. They have inspired leaders to kneel in confession and prayer, to stand up with gospel boldness, and to lead with wisdom and love. And by example and instruction, they have taught entire congregations how to apply scriptural principles to promote reconciliation, peace, and unity.

Their experience and wisdom is set forth in the following pages. I pray that you will study this book carefully and apply its principles in your church with the love and power of Christ. In doing so, you can redeem church conflict, turning it into an opportunity for growth, worship, and kingdom expansion.

Ken Sande, president
Peacemaker Ministries

The Case Study That Still Shocks Us

Since we both have helped thousands of Christians to redeem their conflicts, it's pretty hard to surprise either one of us with a fact pattern or case study. Over the years we have seen the best and the worst responses to conflict from our brothers and sisters in Christ. But the story of one conflicted church, a church we will call Lakeview Community Church, stands out from the rest because of its shocking ending.[1] We will be telling their story in six segments—some background information here as well as our "road map" for helping them redeem their conflicts, one installment at the beginning of each section of the book, and one final segment in the conclusion that you will not want to miss.

How Could This Church Conflict *Ever* Be Redeemed?

God-fearing immigrants founded Lakeview Community Church (LCC) almost one hundred years ago on lakefront property near Cleveland, Ohio. These hardy people shared not only a common faith but common values. They did business with each other, and the children of many of the families married and continued to grow the church and the family businesses.

Over the years the neighborhood around the church's property changed significantly. The new ethnic demographic of the community contributed to the church's growing sense of being disconnected from their immediate neighborhood. In addition, many of the children

13

and grandchildren of the founders lived in more upscale suburbs, but continued to remain members, traveling to the church each Sunday to attend services and visit grandparents. As the grandchildren grew into teens, intergenerational conflicts began to erode the former unity of the church.

On top of all of these changes the church lost their longtime pastor, who had retired in old age and then died. Following his retirement, a series of relatively short pastorates had ended with the present senior pastor taking the church five years ago. This pastor had excellent credentials and experience, and his call to the church was nearly unanimous. Things went pretty well for three years until the church grew to nearly seven hundred and an associate pastor was called. The new associate was fresh out of seminary and eager to serve. It so happened that he was related to one of the founding (and most influential) families in the church.

Conflicts between the senior pastor and the associate pastor began almost immediately. They had extremely divergent views about how LCC should function as a church. In addition, their personalities were polar opposites, so as intergenerational pressures grew, tension between the two pastors also grew. Each began to recruit church members to his side. The senior pastor was focused on serving the existing members, whereas the associate pastor was recruiting those who would focus with him on evangelistic outreach. As a result of the church conflicts, a painful and devastating family conflict grew because the grandparents of the associate pastor strongly supported the senior pastor, but the parents (and wife and children) of the associate pastor strongly supported him. The four generations of this family became further and further estranged as the conflict grew.

One final piece of background: two years earlier, the senior pastor had significantly changed the church governance structure. Historically, the church had followed a strict congregational polity—the congregation voted on virtually everything. But he changed that to an elder-led model where little was decided by the congregation and almost everything was decided by the pastor and elder board. Initially people did not mind this change. But once the conflicts began to grow, *how* decisions were made began to be a major source of conflict.

By the time a team of Christian mediators was hired to help this conflicted church, the situation was a convoluted mess. Members were withholding financial support or leaving the church altogether. Dear friends and even family members who had spent their lifetimes together were no longer speaking with one another. And, of course, the ministry of LCC to its surrounding community was almost nonexistent.

So how was this church conflict *redeemed* by its members? Could both pastors really be happy with *any* result? Could the members be nearly unanimous in the decisions that would ultimately proclaim the gospel of Jesus Christ to their community in one of the most powerful ways we have ever observed? Shockingly, *yes*. And the Acts 15 model for redeeming church conflicts was the "road map" for how it happened.

The Acts 15 Model for Redeeming Church Conflicts

In Acts 15 a serious conflict arose in the early church. God gave those involved great wisdom, and that same wisdom is available to us today. We call this the *Acts 15 model for redeeming church conflicts*, and this model provides the structure for this book.

Perspective. In a church conflict, we can know for certain we have lost perspective if we begin to take conflicts as personal offenses. Conversely, if we see so-called opponents with eyes of compassion, we know God is working in us to redeem the conflict for his glory and our growth.

Discernment. In a church conflict, we know we are on the path of healing discernment if we find ourselves spending more time listening than speaking. Further, as we carefully form and ask questions seeking group health rather than merely advancing a personally favored solution, evidence emerges that God's work of redemption is advancing not only his interests but also our holiness.

Leadership. In a church conflict, if we embrace our personal and individual responsibility for leadership within each of our own personal spheres of influence, we gradually become group problem solvers and increasingly turn away from narrow personal agendas. The more we see ourselves as shepherd-leaders serving others among God's flock, the greater the opportunity for creating an environment from which peace will flow.

Biblical response. In a church conflict, as we remember that Christ loves his church more than we ever will and that he has paid more for it than we ever will, our confidence in the Bible and our commitment to faithful pursuit of biblical responses to conflict will be clear and steadfast. One of the biggest mistakes people make in church conflict is failing to trust Scripture.

In Acts 15 the word *church* refers to *ekklesia*: "the called out" and "the gathered assembly" (see Matt. 16:18). The church is a local group of Christian believers whom God has gathered together to worship him, because his Son, the Lord Jesus Christ, has called them out of the world to be a community of faith.

When we use the word *conflict*, we mean the Peacemaker Ministries' definition of *conflict*: "a difference of opinion or purpose that frustrates someone's goals or desires." This definition allows for the fact that not all conflict is bad, but sometimes conflict can become destructive due to elements of sin, worldliness, and spiritual warfare. Peacemaker Ministries describes these destructive responses to conflict as "escape" and "attack" responses.

Every person has a preferred response to conflict somewhere on the Slippery Slope—see the illustration above—and every church has a *corporate* pattern of response to conflict somewhere on the Slippery Slope.[2] If we are pretending our church conflicts do not exist and are running away from them or attacking others to try to get our way, then we have slipped off the Slippery Slope into destructive, relationship-annihilating, divisive church conflict. *But we don't have to!* We can redeem our church's conflicts. Here is how we define *redeeming church conflict*: Redeeming church conflict means intentional dependence on the humbling and heart-changing grace of Christ's Holy Spirit by turning relational crisis in the church into compassionate care as you take every thought and deed captive to him.

Every church conflict can be redeemed because every church conflict can be used for genuine spiritual growth, both individually and corporately within the body of Christ. Christ can use you to redeem your church's conflict—regardless of how other people respond, even if you are only one lay member out of hundreds or even thousands. You can be God's instrument in redeeming your church's conflicts by following the biblical principles revealed in Holy Scripture, while humbly depending on the Holy Spirit.

A Gentle Warning and Some Encouragement

Church conflict is complex. The various causes of church conflict, the personalities involved, the church's polity, and the level of spiritual maturity among leaders and members will raise questions that no one book or biblical model could possibly address with specificity. Therefore, be *careful* and *pray* as you seek counsel from other church leaders and members about the application of this book and various scriptural passages to your church's specific situation. By seeking counsel from wise and spiritually mature Christians, all of us will hopefully avoid using any part of this book as a weapon to hurt others or to fulfill any sinful goals we might have. Plenty of biblical peacemaking principles have been taken out of context and forced on others in loveless and selfish ways. We pray this will never be the case with this Acts 15 model. Instead, we pray that our efforts in this book will encourage and guide Christians and their churches in redemptive responses to conflicts—responses that are based on the gospel of Jesus Christ. Theologian Dr. Dennis E. Johnson captures the heart of our concern when he writes: "In Scripture the starting point of instruction on right behavior is not a list of our duties, but a declaration of God's saving achievement, bringing us into a relationship of favor with him."[3]

An Important Theological Note

Our model for redeeming church conflict is based on the historical account recorded in Acts 15—a recounting of how the church of the first century redeemed a serious conflict involving Paul, Barnabas, the apostles and elders in Jerusalem, and the Judaizers. In this account of the first church council, it is important to note that the men coming from Judea (referred to later as Judaizers) were believers, although they were doctrinally in error. This dispute, therefore, was not a challenge from unbelievers but a challenge from within. Such disputes are the norm for church conflicts to this day. Rarely do churches split and collapse due to attacks from people outside the church.

We were intentional about structuring the sixteen chapters of this book around the four core principles revealed in Acts 15: *perspective*, *discernment*, *leadership*, and *biblical response*. The first thing we see Paul and Barnabas doing in response to this church conflict is adopting a *perspective* that reflects a clear understanding of who they are and what it means to trust in God. We see them rejoicing in what God is doing among the Gentiles as they respond to the gospel of freedom. Verses 3 and 4 don't report that Paul and Barnabas are overwhelmed by anxiety related to the conflict. No, instead, we see them passing through the land, joyfully telling how the Gentiles are being converted. When they arrive in Jerusalem, they happily report all that God is doing through them. Paul and Barnabas don't succumb to the conflict; they transform and conquer it through their perspective. This contributes to an environment that fosters *discernment*, a search for the truth, not based on any fear but entirely focused on God's interests for his people and the revelation of his Word.

Usually, however, perspective and discernment alone do not lead a church out of conflict. As we see in Acts 15, *leadership* surfaces as the critical next element of this biblical model. Leaders must lead! Peter and James are the leaders who stand before the assembled council and provide the leadership that galvanizes the whole group to respond biblically. Thus shepherd-leaders, responsive to the needs of God's people and absolutely committed to the truth of God's Word, bring unity to the church by leading the church into *biblical responses* to conflict.

This model is *not* a formula. Church conflicts are usually rooted in dozens of differing perspectives and competing desires that are never redeemed or resolved through formulas. Instead, through the Acts 15 model, we are proposing a framework around which a biblical paradigm for group conflict resolution can be built.

Is this use of this portion of God's Holy Word—Acts 15—biblically legitimate, appropriate, and wise? Can it be confidently concluded that this model of responding to church conflicts is appropriately normative for the whole church of all ages and particularly for the church today? When we read about an event or a practice in biblical history of which God approves (see v. 28), should we assume that he wants us to reproduce it today?

We believe so, and here is why. Historical narratives of the Bible differ significantly from other accounts of human history. Second Timothy 3:16–17 states: "All Scripture is God-breathed and is useful for teaching, rebuking, correcting and training in righteousness, so that the man of God may be thoroughly equipped for every good work." In other words, biblical history is not merely human-event history. There is another purpose in view. Dr. Dennis Johnson notes: "It is obvious that we need the light from the church's early days to shine on our churches today."[1] Historical narrative can be used to enlighten our practices within the church today, and this seems particularly appropriate and wise when it comes to responding to church conflicts.

We believe this history, Acts 15, is the history of human events that "must make a difference to our faith and life."[2] We believe this because, as we redeem our conflicts in a manner consistent with the Acts 15 model, we confirm the life-changing message we have heard. This message, of course, is the gospel of Jesus Christ, and, as you will read in this book, this message is the centerpiece for the redemption of church conflicts. The centerpiece of redemption is the "application-belief" in the gospel message as all of its implications are employed in the situation you and your church face. As Professor Johnson states:

> Luke is concerned to write history, to be sure, but he is not writing to satisfy dispassionate historical curiosity. He writes to Theophilus and those like him, who have been catechized in the message of Jesus, but who need a thorough and orderly written account to confirm the life-changing message they have heard. Luke takes his stand in the tradition of biblical narrative—that is, prophetically interpreted history. He writes history that must make a difference to our faith and life.[3]

Therefore, as "prophetically interpreted history," Acts 15 stands biblically, we believe, as a paradigmatic and normative model for the church today.

Every Christian through thoughtful preparation and subsequent action can greatly influence the course of conflicts in their church. Of course, not all of the illustrations we use in this book will apply to all situations. But when the Bible makes statements that are propositionally true, we will be calling Christians to hear them as their Creator's words. Our hope is that all of us will first seek to know what the truth of God's Word is (biblical interpretation) and then act faithfully and consistently with it as we seek to apply this truth to our contemporary situation (biblical application). By doing so, we will be equipped to redeem our church's conflicts as we grow wise in the wisdom that comes from heaven: "The wisdom that comes from heaven is first of all pure; then peace-loving, considerate, submissive, full of mercy and good fruit, impartial and sincere. Peacemakers who sow in peace raise a harvest of righteousness" (James 3:17–18).

Perspective

I make known the end from the beginning, from ancient times, what is still to come. I say: My purpose will stand, and I will do all that I please.

Isaiah 46:10

How do you overcome? You get a breathtaking glimpse of God and the Lamb. You take your eyes off your earthly situation and gaze into heaven and see what true reality looks like. No matter the church's problem, what is most needful is to see God in his glory.

Kevin DeYoung and Ted Kluck

As is the case with many church conflicts involving a senior pastor and an associate pastor, the LCC leadership had initially planned to resolve the conflicts by simply firing the associate pastor. Because the sense of hopelessness and despair was so great at LCC, however, such a move would have alienated nearly half of the congregation and many would have left the church. Fortunately our conflict intervention team had been called before that decision saw the light of day, and a new approach was considered. The first element of that approach was to help the members and leaders of LCC *reassess their perspective* and regain an *eternal perspective* on how these conflicts should be handled.

We did this by gently reminding them of two things: (1) their membership vows, one of which was "to guard the peace, purity, *and unity* of the church," and (2) the stated mission of LCC, which was to fulfill the Great Commission (Matt. 28:18–20). With their hearts refocused *away from* their conflicts and *toward* their shared eternal values (the risen Lord Jesus, their identity in him, their eternal home to come in glory, and their responsibility to proclaim the gospel to their community), they were ready to do the hard work of laboring with Christ to redeem their church's conflicts.

This was a painful process and some members did not persevere—they simply left the church. But the majority stayed and looked intentionally at the reasons the sharp disputes were happening at LCC and what actions, desires, and beliefs were revealed by their conflicts. They did this by seeking wisdom from others (they hired an experienced team of mediators) and quickly they saw that conflict had replaced the Great Commission as the mission of LCC! Shocked by their own loss of eternal perspective, the members began to ask themselves, *Why are we even here as a church?*

One of the most common emotions people feel when facing serious church conflict is hopelessness. Often this is because conflict puts blinders on our eyes and tempts us to isolate ourselves into self-protective groups who agree with us. In our passion to defend our position, we develop tunnel vision that clouds our judgment as we focus our time, energy, and emotions almost exclusively on temporal matters. Things of heaven, theological truths about God and his church, even a passion for bringing the gospel of Jesus Christ to the unsaved, all begin to fade from focus as positions become entrenched in daily battles and we experience despair.

When we are in a conflicted church, our emotions are often similar to those of the psalmist: "My thoughts trouble me and I am distraught. . . . My heart is in anguish within me; the terrors of death assail me. Fear and trembling have beset me; horror has overwhelmed me" (Ps. 55:2, 4–5). These verses reveal strong feelings, much suffering, and the temptation to despair, and many in the midst of church conflict have these same feelings. They are robbed of an accurate, hopeful, God-centered perspective. Rather than confidently living with the hope of the resurrected Christ always before them, rather than being guided and ruled by God's Word, many Christians in conflicted churches begin to act in accordance with their emotions.

As one example of this, I (Tara) served as a mediator in a church where the two main leadership groups (elders and deacons) were barely speaking to one another. At the same time that there were sermons urging their members to love one another, forgive one another, and speak only in edifying ways, these leaders were personally giving in to their hurt and anger. If asked what God's Word said about bitterness and unforgiveness, they could have cited all the appropriate Scriptures. But they had been battling with one another for so long, shoring up their positions by surrounding themselves with people "on their side," that they had lost any sense of God's perspective on their church and their church's conflicts.

In this section, Perspective, we look at how the early church in Acts 15 responded when a severe conflict came into the church. Leaders and members alike maintained an eternal perspective when "sharp disputes" arose, and this perspective guided them every step of the way as they worked to redeem their conflicts.

> Some men came down from Judea to Antioch and were teaching the brothers: "Unless you are circumcised, according to the custom taught by Moses, you cannot be saved." This brought Paul and Barnabas into sharp dispute and debate with them. So Paul and Barnabas were appointed, along with some other believers, to go up to Jerusalem to see the apostles and elders about this question. The church sent them on their way, and as they traveled through Phoenicia and Samaria, they told how the Gentiles had been converted. This news made all the brothers very glad. When they came to Jerusalem, they were welcomed by the church and the apostles and elders, to whom they reported everything God had done through them. (Acts 15:1–4)

In conflict with other believers over theological matters of great importance, Paul, Barnabas, and other believers sought counsel from wise and spiritually mature Christians. They interacted with others to gain a clearer, more accurate, more God-centered perspective on the situation. Yes, they took the conflict seriously. They invested a great amount of time and effort in working through the conflict. And yet, as they journeyed long distances with the great weight of this conflict on them, they told of Gentiles being converted, and this made the brothers glad. They remembered everything God had done and was doing. They did not lose sight of eternity while they were doing the hard job of redemptively working through this church conflict.

We, too, are called to live from such an eternal perspective, interpreting all of life in this world through the lens of one fact: the longest part of our most "real" lives will be lived for eons to come in the perfection of heaven where Christ rules in glory. Right now we live in the in-between, the "already but not yet," but one day we will go home to our heavenly Father's mansion. We live intentionally and consistently with our profession of faith in the present by living with the hope and confidence of this eternal perspective. Otherwise, when suffering and trials come, when we don't get our way, when we are called to bear up under the pain associated with church conflicts, we will not persevere in loving God and loving our neighbor.

This eternal perspective enables us to forgive one another because we remember how great and glorious God is to wretched sinners like us. We marvel at how great a debt we owe and how great a price Christ paid for our salvation. Rather than "biting and devouring" one another (Gal. 5:15), we will remember that the other person involved in this church conflict needs Christ at this time just as much as we do. We are utterly dependent on his grace. And daily we can repent, believe, and rejoice because he has saved us and adopted us as his own. His kingdom will come. He will return in glory to judge the living and the dead. This is guaranteed! So we can have great hope, even in devastating church conflict, as we begin to interpret everything that is happening from the perspective of eternity. We rejoice that even though we may face conflicts now, one day, all of God's children will be perfectly united forever.

A Surprise Mini Case Study

In addition to the ongoing story of Lakeview Community Church, we will be sharing numerous mini case studies throughout the book. These are based on our past conciliation experiences.

One mini case study took us by surprise because it developed *as* we were writing this book and it came not from a conciliation client but from a mutual friend. We had asked her to be a proofreader for the first draft of this manuscript and this is what she wrote us in response: "It is with a heavy, yet encouraged heart that I read through the first draft. You see, I know you didn't know this when you asked me to be a proofreader, but our church is currently weathering some terrible storms of internal conflicts. Since my husband serves as a church leader, I have a close view of how our church, as a general rule, avoids conflicts rather than redeems them. Yes, God's hand has preserved our church from splitting, but damage from painful conflicts continues to grow. Oh, friends, I found myself sighing repeatedly as I read this manuscript. I am so tired and I have been so hurt by all of these conflicts. Yet I know that God is at work and I am confident that he is growing our church family in maturity and a deeper love for Jesus. Thank you for encouraging me to keep my eyes on the Lord. I am grateful for the beautiful truths of biblical peacemaking. Please pray for us. Thank you."

We did pray for this dear friend but we also spent considerable time talking with both her and her husband. We went through many of the principles in this book and, honestly, *their* responses of godliness, faith, and eternal perspective were an encouragement to *us*.

1

When Sharp Disputes
Begin in the Church

If you keep on biting and devouring each other, watch out or you will
be destroyed by each other.

Galatians 5:15

The Devil has many other plans for running your church, all of them
equally insidious. He wants you to get so distracted by internal disputes that you hardly have time to go out and meet people with the
Gospel.

Philip Graham Ryken

The sharp disputes recorded in Acts 15:1–2 are not unique to
the early church and are not rare in the contemporary church.
Church conflicts are frequent and often destructive. You know
what they're like:

- Exhausted after returning home from the annual women's re-
  treat on which you had worked for months, you walk in the
  door only to find three messages from angry church members.
  "Why did you play *that* worship song?" "There was too much
  wasted time!" "There wasn't enough time to slow down and

relax." Your husband encourages you to avoid serving on any women's committee in the future . . .

- You show up for worship Sunday morning and prepare to lead the congregation in singing "Jesus Is Lord" and "We Are One in the Spirit." Everything goes well and you have no idea that during the congregational meeting later that week, an angry faction will demand your resignation as the worship leader. Every decision you've ever made is questioned, scrutinized, and criticized. You look around the room at your so-called friends and begin to plot your escape . . .

- You deliver a heartfelt, God-centered, gospel-proclaiming message to your flock. You pray for them. You love God and you love your sheep. On Monday morning you receive a registered letter informing you that you have been relieved of your pastoral duties and the locks to your church office have been changed. In a flash of fury and embarrassment, you see your education, life's work, and calling disappear. Your wife is terrified. You wonder what went wrong. Sure, you had heard some rumblings; you knew there were some complaints "out there." But this? Fired? You pick up the phone and begin to rally support . . .

- Two families get excited about a certain parenting resource. They recruit other families, and before you know it, two camps exist in the church: "This way is the only way" versus "That way is the wrong way." Many people try to remain neutral, but before long meetings are being held. And then there are meetings *after* the meetings, out in the parking lot of the church (where the *real* meetings always take place). Scripture seems to support both positions. People get louder and more vehement. Issues of character and faith are raised. Families that grew up together, vacationed together, loved God together, now stop interacting with each other . . .

Your church's conflicts may have different facts and themes but the course they take and the damage they cause are always pretty much the same. James describes these "fights and quarrels" as coming from hearts that want something but don't get it; so they "kill and covet" in an effort to get what they want (see James 4:1–3).

Reasons Church Conflicts Often Aren't Redeemed

Throughout this book, when we speak of redeeming church conflict, we hope you will remember that Christ is the true redeemer of his people, our relationships, and our conflicts through his Word and the heart-changing power of his Spirit. Yet Christ enlists us as his co-laborers in the process of peacemaking. Many of us fail to redeem our church conflicts because we are saturated in worldly ideas of what personal relationships are to be rather than grasping what Christ says they are to be as we co-labor with him. The culture says, "Look out for number one!," "Be happy!," "Love those who love you," and "Don't waste your time on toxic or unpleasant people." Often, when difficult relationships develop in the church, we live for our own self-interests and respond as though there were no God. The world's message becomes stronger than the Bible's message for personal living. Too easily we forget whom we are to be co-laboring with and fall into following the ways of this world.

Leaders are not prepared for conflict (even though they should be). Followers are not prepared for conflict (even though they should be). Both leaders and followers are caught in worldliness and many have bought into a postmodern philosophy that says truth is relative and personal and emotive experiences are preeminent. We become passionate, defensive, and self-centered. Rather than studying Scripture and obeying it, we live as a law unto ourselves, motivated by what we want and demand. Rather than a blazing reality, heaven feels vague, so we lose our sense of the nearness of eternity and begin protecting our property, reputations, and comfort in the here and now. Rather than loving God with all our heart, soul, mind, and strength (and loving our neighbor as ourselves), we get tired and distracted and our immediate desires trump eternal realities. Failing to trust in God's sovereignty and living for temporary security, many of us make our church conflicts worse.

Many church members don't read or understand their Bibles, and even those Christians who do know what the Bible says have a hard time trusting its sufficiency for conflict resolution. Ma[ny] never been trained in biblical conflict resolution, but v[e] many secular ideas in schools and workplaces about c[onflict] resolution. Unaware of what the Bible says and grea[tly] by nonbiblical sources, many of us don't realize that the Bible has answers to our conflict-related questions. Secular ideas never lead to "faith expressing itself through love" (Gal. 5:6) because Christ is not at the center of those ideas and the implications of the gospel are ignored.

Even wise and seasoned Christians may jettison their theology when conflicts come. Christians can get locked into personal offenses, lose their perspective, and facilitate only destructive conversations. The old statement "Sin makes us stupid" could be restated as "Church conflict makes us utterly stupid." Even the most intelligent, astute, biblical Christian will be tempted to look "stupid" when facing church conflict. As mediators, we have sat between great theologians, who could run circles around us intellectually, and we can describe with great detail what it looks like to see their theological training and maturity melt down under the fire of relational strife. Bright, caring Christians can act like dull, loveless people when they are attacked and accused, threatened and rejected. Left to their own devices, no matter how high their IQ or how many degrees they have earned, many Christians will either run away from church conflict or exacerbate it. Helping conflicted Christians come back to their senses is not easy but it is possible. The first step is to put your trust in God when sharp disputes begin in the church.

Put Your Trust in God

If most people in conflicted churches were polled and asked if God is trustworthy, the majority would probably respond, "Of course!" But the overwhelming dynamic in church conflict is not one of trusting God. Instead, we tend to follow this downward spiral:

- We think our evaluation of the situation is always right.
- Rather than treating people as God treats us, we disdain the perspectives of others and treat them with contempt and disrespect.
- We think God is on our side and we have God's attention, care, and blessing more than our opponents do.
- We become defensive and condemn others because we believe that God takes our side and condemns them too.

- Our lives are marked by pride and selfishness rather than humility and love.

This dynamic reminds us of country and western singer Johnny Lee's lyric, "looking for love in all the wrong places." In church conflicts, Christians are "looking for trust in all the wrong places," because they are trusting in their own perceptions.

As trust breaks down, communications falter. Incomplete and inaccurate information seeps out, uncharitable presumptions begin to reign, and people stop trusting God and one another. Fear and prayerlessness combine with our natural inclination toward self-protection and before we know it, we really trust in only one thing: *ourselves*.

As one example of this, we served on a team intervening in a church where, as in the LCC case study, one of the main issues was a conflict between the senior pastor and the associate pastor. By the end of our eleven days on-site at the church, many of the people involved had made much progress. Even the pastors had made confessions and granted forgiveness. Things seemed hopeful at the time, but the story was quite different when the team leader checked in with them a few weeks later: "I know I've forgiven him. I'm trying to rebuild the relationship. But I just don't *trust* him."

Lack of trust is the common denominator in all church conflicts. Even after words of forgiveness, it takes time to clear away the rubble of broken relationships and rebuild a firm foundation of trust. This is particularly true for church conflicts that have simmered and stewed for years. If care is not given, an unhealed breach of trust will keep the wound of conflict open and vulnerable to further infection.

So how do Christians rebuild trust with one another in the aftermath of church conflict, even if problems have been resolved and words of reconciliation spoken? The parable of the Pharisee and the tax collector found at Luke 18:9–14 is instructive. While the parable addresses the problem of seeing self-righteousness as the path to right standing before God, it is equally a pattern for recovery from the effects of church conflict.

To some who were confident of their own righteousness and looked down on everybody else, Jesus told this parable: "Two men went up to the temple to pray, one a Pharisee and the other a tax collector. The Pharisee stood up and prayed about himself: 'God, I thank you that I am not like other men—robbers, evildoers, adulterers—or even like this tax collector. I fast twice a week and give a tenth of all I get.'

"But the tax collector stood at a distance. He would not even look up to heaven, but beat his breast and said, 'God, have mercy on me, a sinner.'

"I tell you that this man, rather than the other, went home justified before God. For everyone who exalts himself will be humbled, and he who humbles himself will be exalted."

Humility is the healing balm for the continuing malady of the loss of trust. Genuine humility calls us to put our trust in God, not in our own hearts. Our knowledge and evaluation of our church's situation is imperfect. It is folly to put all of our trust in ourselves: "He who trusts in himself is a fool" (Prov. 28:26). "Lean not on your own understanding" (Prov. 3:5).

Humility seeks relationship with former combatants. Rather than putting our trust in people who agree with us and affirm only our perspectives and our convictions, humility calls us to seek counsel from people of varying perspectives. But Scripture also warns us not to place ultimate trust in other people. "This is what the LORD says: 'Cursed is the man who trusts in man, who depends on flesh for his strength'" (Jer. 17:5). Even the counsel of like-minded friends must submit to the priority of God's principles.

True humility trusts in God; the focus of the humble person is the Lord. Through faith, we are called to give God our worries, fears, and doubts. We can trust that he is the Redeemer who will right every wrong in this life or in the life to come—for every wrong has either already been paid for at the cross, or will be paid for in hell. Therefore, we can turn away from any spiritual unfaithfulness related to vengeance and prize Jesus above even our own vindication! We trust in that which is unseen more than in that which is seen (see Heb. 11:1). We determine what would please and honor God and then we do it. Trusting God is our only truly safe haven. "Blessed is the man who trusts in the LORD, whose confidence is in him" (Jer. 17:7). "It is better to take refuge in the LORD than to trust in man. It is better to take refuge in the LORD than to trust in princes" (Ps. 118:8–9).

To trust in God is to grow in spiritual maturity. When we trust God, we pray. When we trust God, we stop valuing the things that the world values (comfort, success, recognition, fame) and we begin to value the things that Jesus values (sacrifice, service, humility, love). We start to view ourselves just as Paul saw himself, the worst of all sinners (see 1 Tim. 1:15), and we throw ourselves at the feet of Jesus and wash his feet with our tears. Our weeping comes, but we have the hope of joy in the morning. When we are living by humble trust in God, we overflow with love for our neighbor and our enemy. Then, when we see our fellow brothers and sisters also trusting God, we can begin to trust each other again as well. Trusting God, *especially while we are in the midst of conflict*, is indispensable to redeeming church conflict because it opens to us the reality of again being able to trust others.

God Is Still at Work

No matter the level of conflict in our church, God is still at work. It may be seen in a youth program that is still going strong and bringing people to the Lord on a regular basis; it may be seen in an overseas mission or an inner-city mentoring program. More than likely, there is some church ministry that clearly reveals how God is still at work. We can celebrate these "blessed" ministries as stepping-stones toward reconciliation and unity. What would it look like for us to focus gratefully on what is right in the church and use those aspects of church life as an encouragement to everyone involved?

As our focus shifts away from our church's conflicts and toward what God is doing, and as we celebrate his work in our church, our fearful hearts will be quieted and our propensity to run away or attack will be lessened. If even one or two other people in our church likewise experience this reorientation of focus and perspective, we can be united around a common vision, passion, and mission—*the glory of God*. Rather than seeking to control the situation, we can trust that God will give us everything we need for life and godliness through Jesus Christ (2 Peter 1:3). He does this through his grace: the Holy Spirit, Christ himself interceding for us, the living and active Word of God, our baptism, the Lord's Supper, and the counsel of other wise and spiritually mature Christians.

When the clouds of conflict roll in, we tend to forget all that God has already done for us in Jesus. Ultimately, doubt about who God is, what he has done, and what he is doing lies at the heart of conflict among Christians. Such doubt is a result of unbelief. The last thing our church needs when responding to conflict is Christians expressing any degree of unbelief in God. But when we remember that all of history is on a trajectory of redemption, we will have hope because no matter the darkness of sin, the reality of spiritual warfare, or the suffering associated with life in a fallen world, the wrong *will* fail. The right *will* prevail. It is certain because it is based on all of God's promises; it is based on the faithfulness of God as we have seen in the resurrection of Christ and the provision of the Holy Spirit (Eph. 1:13–14).

What we hope for is a certainty when we hope for what is consistent with God's will. Our hope is founded on the conviction that God will fulfill his promises to us. Nothing can thwart God's perfect redemptive plan, and we can celebrate this truth even while we are in heartbreaking church conflict. This is not pie-in-the-sky psychobabble or a naive rose-colored-glasses perspective. This is biblical truth. God is clinging to us with a grip that will never let go.

Apply This to Your Church Conflict

At the beginning of Acts 15, we see the words that caused conflict: "Unless you are circumcised, according to the custom taught by Moses, you cannot be saved." These words, spoken by men who believed in Jesus as the long-promised Messiah of God, confronted Paul and Barnabas as they taught a contrary message in the church at Antioch. The Judaizers, Jewish believers confused about the gospel's message of salvation by grace alone through faith alone in Christ alone, were throwing the early church into confusion. The gospel's message was the good news of salvation through belief in Jesus Christ, the only Son of God, who paid the penalty for the sins of mankind, period! No additions! No circumcision! No observance of any tradition of Moses or otherwise! The Judaizers brought conflict to the church, and Paul and Barnabas opposed them.

Consider how the conflicts at your church may have similarities to the "sharp disputes" recorded in Acts 15:

- *Internal participants.* The conflict started among people of faith in the church. Church conflicts are rarely the product of an attack from the outside. Church conflicts are usually "family matters."
- *Material difference.* The conflict is over differences represented by separate groups. In Acts 15 the difference is over a matter of Christian doctrine. Is a person saved by grace alone through faith alone in Jesus Christ alone, or are there additional requirements? Paul and Barnabas taught that there were no additions. The positions taken in this Acts 15 conflict are mutually exclusive. One is doctrinally wrong. Your church's present conflicts may not be over a matter of doctrine, but most likely the dynamics of your conflicts represent a difference over a favored church tradition. It could be anything from a preferred worship style to a controversy over the pastor's personality. It could reflect a favored preference or opinion or it could be sin based, reflecting hardness of heart contrary to the teaching and standards of Holy Scripture.
- *Emotionally invested responses.* Participants in the conflict are emotionally invested in the outcome. Often they view conflict as a fight for "truth" that requires one side to yield. Many church conflicts are fueled by the belief that the opposing side must be defeated. In Acts 15 the conflict is laden with emotion and characterized by men with strong views and strong personalities on both sides. Verse 2 states that Paul and Barnabas were brought into "sharp dispute and debate" with the Judaizers. In Philippians 3:2 Paul calls the Judaizers "dogs, those men who do evil, those mutilators of the flesh." The people involved in your church's conflicts are probably also expressing emotion-driven positions. Usually anger, harshness, sarcasm, bitterness, and similar emotions accompany church conflict. At this stage, conflict quickly escalates and becomes an *emotionally invested personal* matter as much as it ever was a *material* conflict (such as a difference over some tradition, doctrine, practice, or personality).

Now that we have described common elements of church conflict—internal participants, a material difference, and emotionally invested responses—let's consider the next steps of the Acts 15 model for redeeming your church's present conflicts. As we do so, our prayer is that no matter how overwhelming or exhausting your church conflict may be, you will be strengthened and encouraged, according to God's Word, as you put your hope and confidence in the Lord Jesus Christ: "My soul is weary with sorrow; strengthen me according to your word" (Ps. 119:28).

We pray that you will be hopeful as you remember who you are in Christ. We pray you will be able to trust others again as you all trust what God has done for you. And from that saving grace, we pray you will have the encouragement and courage required to live according to God's Word when sharp disputes arise in your church.

Questions for Reflection

1. How are your church's present conflicts similar to the conflict described in Acts 15? How are they dissimilar?
2. Are you addressing the conflicts in your church from an eternal perspective? What hard evidence indicates that you are doing so?
3. Considering the structure of Acts 15 as a model for redeeming church conflict, what hope do you have for redeeming your church's present conflicts? On what foundation do you ground that hope?

Recommended Resources for Further Study

Mark Driscoll, *Doctrine: What Christians Should Believe* (Wheaton: Crossway, 2010).

Dennis Johnson, *The Message of Acts in the History of Redemption* (Phillipsburg, NJ: P&R Publishing, 1997).

C. J. Mahaney, *The Cross Centered Life: Keeping the Gospel the Main Thing* (Sisters, OR: Multnomah, 2002).

David Powlison, *Power Encounters: Reclaiming Spiritual Warfare* (Grand Rapids: Baker, 1995).

2

Seeking the Wisdom of Others—
Is That Wise?

The whole body, joined and held together by every supporting ligament, grows and builds itself up in love, as each part does its work.

Ephesians 4:16

You are where you are because that is where God wants you. He put
you with the Christians around you because they are the kind you
need and you are the kind they need. . . . Do not reject God's instruments. He knows what you need better than you do.

Ray Stedman

When the early church at Antioch was facing a serious
conflict, its members made a wise decision to seek assistance from other spiritually mature Christians: "So
Paul and Barnabas were appointed, along with some other believers, to go up to Jerusalem to see the apostles and elders about this
question" (Acts 15:2).

One of the first things we should consider when we begin the
journey of redeeming our church's conflict is how we might benefit
from involving others. This may be something as simple as prayerfully reflecting on biblically faithful, Christ-centered resources from
Christians who have experience in biblical conflict resolution and

then faithfully obeying all that Scripture calls us to do. It may mean reaching out to wise and spiritually mature people within our church or denomination or, if our church is an independent church, to other gifted and wise Christians in our community.

Sadly, this idea of getting help by involving others in church conflicts is usually not a step that church leaders and members take readily. Instead, conflict tends to isolate people. Rather than humbly seeking help at the first signs of conflict, many people either run away and avoid the conflict entirely or hunker down in isolated camps and lob relational bombs from behind walls of self-protection (the *escape* and *attack* responses on the Slippery Slope—see diagram on page 16).

Wisdom, however, is not found in isolation through running away or attacking, but in the counsel of many (Prov. 15:22). Even though we may be able to work through some conflicts with *personal peacemaking responses* (such as overlooking offenses, reconciliation/discussion, and negotiation), many times we need to get help by involving others. Peacemaker Ministries describes the "involving others" responses to conflict as the *assisted peacemaking responses* (mediation, arbitration, and accountability/church discipline).

There are many reasons that it may be wise to involve others in our church conflicts:

- We cannot readily see our own blind spots—but others frequently have a clearer perspective on what is happening because they are not emotionally invested. They have not been telling themselves the conflict story over and over again, which can lead to distortion. They can hear several perspectives and are not invested in one perspective being right.
- When our hearts are weighed down with crushing burdens, it can be hard to remember anything that is lovely, excellent, admirable, or praiseworthy (see Phil. 4:8)—but others can help us remember truth because their hearts are not the ones being battered.
- Fear is a powerful emotion. When we are afraid that we may be losing control of a situation or about to lose something of great value to us, our judgment can become skewed. We may give in to defensive and self-righteous attitudes or actions and

not even realize it—but wise and mature Christians can help us see our sin and repent.

- The presence of an impartial third party can help hold tempers under control and help conflicted people agree on fundamental rules of fairness.
- A neutral third party can encourage us when all seems hopeless and lost. He or she can carry us, believe with us, and remind us of the sure foundation and hope that is ours in Christ. This person can help us remember to put our individual conflicts in a broader context—the context of eternity.

Most Christian churches have as a membership vow something like the following: "I acknowledge that I am a sinner in the sight of God, justly deserving his displeasure, and without hope except in his sovereign mercy in Christ Jesus." Such a pronouncement is usually the first statement made by a person seeking admission into the visible church. In other words, we each acknowledge we are a mess without hope *unless we have the assistance of another.* And yet when we come to the point of conflict in the church, our first response is often denial and neglect—we pretend that we do not have any problems or we assume our problems will resolve themselves on their own. Rather than acknowledging our corporate sin and great need of help, we circle the wagons and huddle as though we can figure everything out on our own without the assistance of another.

Tragically, in many conflicted churches, this delay in reaching out for help means that enough time has passed since the conflict began that the pastor has fled or been forced out, many leaders have left, and the congregation has experienced some form of mass exodus—*all without ever reaching out for help.*

Furthermore, one of the greatest mistakes churches make when confronting churchwide conflict is initially to downplay the seriousness of the situation and so fail to ask for help. Because of hiding and delay, conflicts grow deeper and more serious. For example, in the course of one conflicted church intervention case that I (Dave) served on, I met for an extended period with the former pastor who had been forced to leave. The conflict had started over changes in worship style. At first it seemed merely a low grumble among a small group of older members. He believed that as time went by these people would gradually get used to the new pattern and the new music. That didn't happen and people began to drift away. The church's leaders did not take much notice and had no "exit interview" process, which would have given them valuable feedback. Also they failed to hold people accountable to their membership vows, that they would seek first to resolve any conflict peacefully, so the drift continued and gradually accelerated. When the significance of the impact on the church's income became noticeable, it was already too late. The conflict began to take on a life of its own as the recriminations began in earnest.

The former pastor told me how clear it all was in hindsight but how blind and foolish he and other leaders had been at the beginning. They had ignored the two or three who had the courage to come to the leadership with their concerns. They had been so focused on the "newness" of what they were doing that they hid their heads in the proverbial sand and failed to address the concerns. This broken man grieved that he had not acted quickly to provide a fair, responsive, and impartial process for the airing and addressing of complaints. In hindsight, he realized how much people had been hurt because their voice had not been heard. I grieved with this man because I knew that his ministry at this church would have been saved and the grief of so much conflict avoided had he and other leaders addressed complaints at the right time.

Biblical Peacemaking Resources

Although many of us understand the importance of studying Scripture and testing the counsel of others against the Word of God, we may feel unsure of our abilities due to a lack of training or experience in dealing with biblical peacemaking. We may know biblical principles like "love your enemy" and "forgive seventy-seven times," but many of us have never learned how to apply those principles when we are facing actual conflicts.

We can be thankful that wise men and women have gone before us and not only have they studied the biblical principles related to peacemaking (such as repentance, confession, confrontation, and forgiveness), they have applied these principles in countless real-life situations and then written about the results. Your own denomination or conference may have specific peacemaking resources that would be of benefit to any church facing conflict.[1]

The Bible presents a systematic way of looking at and responding to interpersonal conflict. God has a very high priority for peaceful relationships between his eternal offspring. This is what Paul is communicating when he says in Ephesians 4:3 to "make *every* effort" to maintain peace. He is encouraging just that—make every effort—not just a halfhearted attempt. But the effort we are to make is not one based simply on our own personal opinions, preferences, notions, or ideas. God calls us to make an effort that is consistent with what he has revealed. If we were to do a careful study of the key biblical passages on interpersonal relationships interrupted by conflict, we would discover that God loves us enough not to leave such an important topic to our chance interpretation or application. No, he is very specific, methodical, and procedural.

Take for example Matthew 5:21–26. In this portion of what we call the Sermon on the Mount, Jesus addresses the matter of interpersonal relationships, starting with a discussion of the commandment not to murder. But the discussion goes far beyond the act of taking another's life. Getting to the foundational heart motivation of a murderous act, Jesus says, "Anyone who is angry with his brother will be subject to judgment" (v. 22). Anger plays a part in virtually every conflict, and Jesus moves quickly to the point of addressing our anger (our heart's motivation) before it results in an overt act: "If you are offering your gift at the altar and there remember that your brother has something against you, leave your gift there in front of the altar. First go and be reconciled to your brother; then come and offer your gift" (vv. 23–24).

Before we can worship properly, God, who knows our every thought, feeling, and emotion, tells us, first, to get our relationships with our fellow worshipers right. Our anger destroys our worship. Our anger leads to death (spiritual and/or physical). God tells us *what* to do (be reconciled) and then *why* (the consequences will escalate if we don't—see verses 23–26)! Unresolved anger leads to unintended consequences. God has a system for resolving conflicts that have shattered his children's relationships, and we ignore it at our peril. (See also the patterns of Matt. 18:15–20; 1 Cor. 6:1–8; and Gal. 6:1–2.)

Ken Sande, author of *The Peacemaker*, calls a summary of a thorough, systematic means of personal conflict resolution the Four Gs.[2] Each G stands for the first word of each of four elements essential to conflict resolution. When in conflict:

1. Glorify God.
2. Get the log out of your eye.
3. Gently restore.
4. Go and be reconciled.

These four "steps" provide for us a guide for remembering a biblical and systematic approach to conflict resolution and have been applied by thousands of Christians to resolve their interpersonal conflicts. In section 4 of this book we will return to these elements and look at them from the perspective of how they can be applied to group conflicts, particularly in light of our Acts 15 model. For now, take confidence that such tools for the intentional and systematic resolution of conflicts are biblically based and ordained by God for our profitable use.

As we prayerfully consider involving others in our church's conflicts, we ought to know the theology and the theological convictions of our church. We should also know the polity—how our church is organized and governed and what the Bible says about how our church is to be organized and governed. And before we listen to the counsel of anyone, we should know his or her theology and polity.[3] (Appendix B discusses in depth what should be considered before engaging a third-party church conflict consultant.)

 In our experience, the church that turns first to a study of the *biblical* process of conflict resolution rarely finds it necessary to deal with the many collateral conflicts generally associated with the tension caused by the core issues of the conflict. Significant material issues may need to be answered, but the way these issues are resolved changes radically once people begin to deal biblically with each other in their personal relationships. So, rather than focusing on the issues at hand and potential steps to address them, first focus on the *biblical process* of conflict resolution. This approach has two positive results:

1. It appropriately directs people involved to the issue of *how* conflict is to be dealt with (biblical process).
2. It provides the breathing room needed to step back from the conflict itself so there is time to gain perspective.

The procedural study in effect deals substantively with the hearts of those in conflict. Thus, before we address any material issues of the conflict, we are to take the time to study God's Word and discover his process. Once we have done so, we will see more clearly if and how we should reach out to others for further assistance.

Seeking Counsel within Our Church

There may be people within the church who can assist us with our conflicts. We should use caution, however, because one of the most insidious and destructive aspects of church conflict is *gossip*. People have an innate desire to be in the know, and when rumors of conflicts begin to spread in a church, half-truths, uncharitable presumptions, and outright lies can tear a church in two. Thus we are to be particularly careful *not to gossip* and *not to slander* if we decide to involve others and seek counsel within our own church. Keep in mind Proverbs 16:28: "A perverse man stirs up dissension, and a gossip separates close friends."

The following questions are helpful to consider as we evaluate whether involving others from within the church would be redemptive or destructive.

1. Have I made a sincere and concerted effort to resolve this conflict as privately as possible?
2. Is it absolutely necessary that I share this information? Is there any way for me to seek counsel without going into specifics that might cast another person or group in a negative light?
3. Am I seeking counsel from a spiritually mature, trustworthy person who is not a gossip or slanderer? Can I trust him or her theologically and relationally?
4. What is my motivation for involving others? Am I seeking to bolster my position and strengthen my "camp" in this church

conflict? Or am I seeking God's glory, the unity of the saints, and a wise resolution of the material aspects of this conflict?

5. Being personally objective, is my reputation one that is consistent with being a safe person—that is, not a gossip and one to be trusted with sensitive information?

If the responses to such questions indicate that we have God-honoring, love-of-neighbor, peace-promoting motivations for involving others, then we ought to do so—prayerfully and carefully. It can be wise to seek counsel from a spiritually mature person who can direct us in our studies of Scripture related to the current conflict. This person should be trustworthy, and as we have said, not a gossip or busybody. Ideally, he or she will have a thorough, biblical theology for conflict resolution and be able to guide appropriately. We should see the fruits of "faith expressing itself through love" (Gal. 5:6) in his or her life—a love for God and neighbor. This person should be a true peacemaker: willing to confess, eager to forgive, not afraid to gently confront when necessary. Even in emotionally charged situations, this person should keep a level head and not be prone to angry outbursts.

By seeking counsel and assistance from wise and spiritually mature people within the church, we will grow in maturity, help others to grow, and help our church reflect Ephesians 4:16: "The whole body, joined and held together by every supporting ligament, grows and builds itself up in love, as each part does its work."

Involving People outside Our Church

When positions have polarized, trust has been demolished, and a church is stuck in intractable conflict, it is important that all of her leaders and members remember that they are all part of something larger than merely their local congregation. Even if no one in the local church will be accepted by all sides as an impartial peacemaker, there may be denominational resources that could be helpful. In addition, independent churches are part of the universal church and may rightly call on the resources of other churches for help. This may mean seeking counsel and advice from wise and experienced

Christians in the community. It may mean hiring professional mediators. The people to whom we reach out for help should not only have sufficient maturity and experience to identify and understand what is happening in our church conflict and the reasons behind it, but also have sufficient theological training to help us see objectively all aspects of the conflict from a biblical perspective.

Churches are never alone. But so often, in their embarrassment and pride, they stay alone when facing conflict. Rather than living out a chief kingdom characteristic of genuine humility (see Matt. 18:4), many conflicted churches, to keep up the appearance of "success," cut themselves off from the resource of other wise and gifted people. It does not have to be that way. If our church needs outside assistance, humble, experienced, qualified mediators and consultants can be the strategic help required.

Apply This to Your Church Conflict

Many church leaders and members may be embarrassed by the fact they have conflict. They may readily acknowledge the effect and consequences of sin in their personal lives, but somehow it seems that when they see it affecting the health of their church, they want to minimize or ignore the fact that the same dynamic is at work. This may be due to ignorance and immaturity, but often it is due to pride.

Pride drives us to overlook our own sin while, for the sake of winning, we quickly look for and find the faults of others. Pride motivates us to guard the reputation of the church to outsiders, even a false reputation, more than we guard the relationships already within the church. Pride skews our focus to numeric growth in attendance and financial donations, rather than to the maturing of faithful, involved members of the church.

Ironically, pride seeks to protect reputation but then ends up destroying reputation as Christians and unbelievers in the community watch the members of a church battle one another to the point of divisiveness and potentially even closure of the church. By isolating themselves and refusing to involve others, proud Christians lose what they had sought to preserve—unity.

Consider just a few of the costs of church conflict when leaders and members fail to address it in a biblically faithful manner:[4]

- God is dishonored and the growth of his kingdom is slowed.
- Families and friendships are broken.
- Individual sanctification is impeded.
- Ministry projects are delayed, rendered ineffective, or canceled.
- The church's reputation and witness are diminished and evangelism is weakened.
- Staff and volunteer time and energy are diverted or wasted.
- Members reduce or withhold financial support or leave the church.
- Much time and money is spent recruiting, hiring, and training new staff.
- Pastors or church workers leave the ministry altogether.
- And more . . .

Such destructive results from unresolved conflict should make us flee pride, disregard the fear of man, and turn from defensiveness and self-righteousness. As we resist these temptations and refuse to hide our disagreements, we can redeem church conflict through prayer, study, and the spiritual resources provided by Christ. Furthermore, involving others may help us walk through the refining fire of church conflict rather than being devoured by the consuming fire of uncontrolled passions.

Questions for Reflection

1. Have you felt isolated as your church deals with its present conflicts? How so?
2. How would you explain to a fellow church member the relationship between your personal dependence on Christ and the church's need to depend on other Christians as the difficulties of conflict are confronted?
3. In what ways are you personally involved in your church's present conflicts? Is there a trustworthy Christian friend you could

speak with about your involvement? If so, in what manner will you approach him or her to avoid gossip?

Recommended Resources for Further Study

Timothy S. Lane and Paul David Tripp, *How People Change* (Greensboro, NC: New Growth Press, 2008).

David Powlison, *Seeing with New Eyes: Counseling and the Human Condition through the Lens of Scripture* (Phillipsburg, NJ: P&R Publishing, 2003).

Jim Van Yperen, *Making Peace: A Guide to Overcoming Church Conflict* (Chicago: Moody, 2002).

3

....

Eternity Makes a Difference

Blessed is the man who trusts in the LORD, whose confidence is in him.

Jeremiah 17:7

Real change comes in people's attitudes toward conflict and reconciliation through a renewed vision of the Gospel of Jesus Christ.

Alfred Poirier

As you consider your church's conflicts, where is your focus? How much time do you currently spend rejoicing in the Lord and praying with hope? And how much time do you spend worrying?

When a church is degenerating into serious, destructive conflict, it can be hard for members and leaders to remember the truth about God and his church. As circumstances feel overwhelming and hopeless, it is normal to focus energy, time, and emotions on the conflicted issues, rather than on worshiping God. Sometimes, in our doubt, worry, and fear, we may be tempted to forget the character of God, the purpose of the church, and the resources that we have in Christ. With a biblically faithful view of God, and a heart of faith and trust in him, we can choose to celebrate and rejoice in the positive things happening in our local church, even while conflicts exist. This right worship of God and a focus on eternity as a present reality and future hope will help us overcome our fears and doubts.

The early church provides an excellent model of this focus on God and his eternally important works that are being revealed in the present.

> The church sent them on their way, and as they traveled through Phoenicia and Samaria, they told how the Gentiles had been converted. This news made all the brothers very glad. When they came to Jerusalem, they were welcomed by the church and the apostles and elders, to whom they reported everything God had done through them. (Acts 15:3–4)

Even though the conflict was serious and they could have spent all of their time worrying and in debate over the material issues and positions, Paul and Barnabas chose to tell about "the miraculous signs and wonders God had done" (v. 12); they "reported everything God had done" (v. 4). Focusing on the positive in this way and rejoicing in what the Lord is doing to change lives and grow the church is not "name it and claim it" bad theology. It is addressing temporal issues in a church conflict with a God-centered heart and a God-centered trust.

Focusing on God and celebrating God's eternal work in our church provide sources of joy, hope, and encouragement when we are in conflict. This perspective also gives us, and all of the members of our church, unity around a common vision, passion, and mission; it helps make sense of the conflicts so as to bear up under them. Also, because conflict is so discouraging and all-encompassing, we may even begin to believe lies (such as God has abandoned us because we just can't seem to get through these issues). Seeing evidence of his grace will comfort us, reminding us that he is still with us and that he is passionately at work in his church full of sinners saved by grace. Also the evidence shows us that his gospel is powerful and triumphant, and as we carry these truths with us back into the conflict, it will bolster our hope.

Remembering God's Attributes

Christianity is built on the fact that God has revealed himself in very specific ways for very specific purposes and that revelation is by human beings. Although postmodernists deny propositional truth about God and his plan for mankind, God's Word has proven to be reliable, trustworthy, and sufficient for living life and enduring conflict.

As you consider the details of your church conflict, it may feel as if things are out of control, but they are not. They are not in *your* control, but they are in *God's* control. You may have a hard time feeling very safe or protected right now—especially if important things are on the line in your church conflict (theological concerns, staffing decisions, matters of mission and morality). When you think about your church conflicts, it may feel very dark and uncomfortable. But just as Psalm 57 reminds us, you are tucked under the very wing of God. You are ultimately safe and secure because Jesus has deprived the world of its power to hurt you *ultimately* (Josh. 1:5; Prov. 29:25; Luke 12:4–7; Heb. 13:5). Someone bigger and stronger than you is in control. Never forget the God behind the scenes, for his attributes and character will see you through the conflict. Remember the character of God. He is:

- Supreme
- Sovereign
- Holy
- Powerful
- Immutable
- Faithful
- Patient
- Merciful
- Gracious
- Loving
- Good
- And so much more!

To redeem our church's conflicts, we need a *bigger fear* than the one driven by any temporal conflict—a holy, righteous fear of God that is reverent and supremely respectful. Usually fear of conflict reflects our fear of the potential but unknown consequences of conflict (loss of control, loss of a favored tradition, and so on), whereas the holy fear of God assures us of known consequences: peace with him and a greater dependency on his Word that communicates his promises for our eternal well-being. In the words of pastor and well-known Bible teacher Thabiti Anyabwile:

> Members of Christian churches continue to think small thoughts of God and great thoughts of man. This state of affairs reveals that too many Christians have neglected their first great calling: to know their God. Every Christian is meant to be a theologian in the best and most intimate sense of the word.[1]

When we see God as we should see him, we will appropriately fear him more than anything or anyone else, just as Moses did in Exodus 3:6: "Then he said, 'I am the God of your father, the God of Abraham, the God of Isaac and the God of Jacob.' At this, Moses hid his face, because he was afraid to look at God."

An eternal perspective that overflows with appropriate and reverent fear of God pushes out any fear of our church conflict. As we fear God more and trust and love him more, we will also have more love in our hearts for our neighbors because *perfect love drives out fear.* "There is no fear in love. But perfect love drives out fear, because fear has to do with punishment. The one who fears is not made perfect in love" (1 John 4:18).

Angry people are often fearful people. Focused on accomplishing narrow goals and defending a selfish perspective, angry people may fear failure, embarrassment, or losing out on self-centered priorities. When we are angry, we may have extensively footnoted documents "proving" we are right, with biblical citations and facts galore; but rarely do we make a priority of valuing God's commands to love our neighbor (see Matt. 19:19) and to be reconciled (see Matt. 5:24). Many times in a church conflict, anger masks a swirling vortex of fear—the loss of control, the ruin of reputations, financial catastrophe, and/or theological error. The list of possible things to fear is endless, but the one thing we ought to fear is usually absent. In most protracted, difficult church conflicts, the fear of God is rarely present. Instead we finite human beings respond in our own limited strength and thus, sensing our own weakness, we may respond in self-protective, faithless ways. For example, we may run away, attack, seek to manipulate or control, and forget about God altogether. When we do so, we sound a lot like Moses when God said to him: "'So now, go. I am sending you to Pharaoh to bring my people the Israelites out of Egypt.' But Moses said to God, 'Who am I, that I should go to Pharaoh and bring the Israelites out of Egypt?'" (Exod. 3:10–11).

Even after God's revelation of who he is and all that he will do for Moses and the Israelites, Moses is still seeking to run away and avoid the conflict. Initially Moses makes excuses, and by doing so he represents most Christians who have been overwhelmed by the complexity of church conflict. "Moses answered, 'What if they do not believe me or listen to me and say, "The LORD did not appear to you"?'" (Exod. 4:1).

The thought of actually engaging with the people involved in church conflict may be terrifying to us. We may echo the words of Moses: "They will not believe me or listen to me." And they may not. Angry people, especially Christians in conflicted churches, want what they want rather than what God wants for their church. Just as law enforcement officials know that the most dangerous situations they face are domestic disturbances because people involved in those conflicts don't respond in rational ways, any experienced Christian mediator will tell you that church conflicts frequently yield the same depth of irrational emotion and intensity. In the family of God, where the most intimate and long-lasting relationships have been nurtured and are now threatened, the emotions are close and personal; the hurt can devastate beyond rationality and reason; and the responses, even of godly, mature Christians, can frequently go overboard and become irrational.

But God is still in control. We can argue with him all we like and offer our excuses, as Moses did. "Moses said to the LORD, 'O Lord, I have never been eloquent, neither in the past nor since you have spoken to your servant. I am slow of speech and tongue'" (v. 10). We can try to weasel out of our responsibilities: "O Lord, please send someone else to do it" (v. 13). But God is relentless and he is on the move. He is sovereign and he is at work, softening and hardening hearts: "The LORD said to Moses, 'When you return to Egypt, see that you perform before Pharaoh all the wonders I have given you the power to do. *But I will harden his heart so that he will not let the people go'"* (v. 21).

God's work may feel obscure and mysteriously unknowable in church conflicts. You may feel overwhelmed and without power to bring about any positive result, but the God of all creation is at work. Focusing on this brings the hope of redemption to even the most devastating of church conflicts. For example, I (Tara) assisted a church where a father had molested his daughter. Talk about a seemingly hopeless situation! Leaders and members alike were striving to discern how to minister to the man (even as he faced appropriate criminal prosecution) and to the daughter (who was, of course, severely affected by his evil actions). Complex counseling, church discipline, and legal issues abounded. And yet there was hope because God was present and at work. God still cares for his people just as he did in the time of Moses. His love for his people is an eternal truth—a given. Nothing can change it or thwart it, even when horrific suffering impacts our lives.

Redeeming church conflict is less about resolving specific problems than it is about seeing conflict as a means by which God is growing his people into true saints, true eternal children who are being continuously conformed to his holy image. Christians are eternal beings with a significant eternal future. Having to deal with a church conflict is one way we are being weaned away from earthly confidence and moved toward a preoccupation with Christ alone. Sometimes, when people stubbornly refuse to submit to God's Word and do not "make every effort to keep the unity of the Spirit through the bond of peace" (Eph. 4:3), when they refuse to listen to counsel and insist on arguing and fighting (often irrationally and without even a shred of love), they are merely forgetting they are children of God. At other times, their sinful responses may simply be revealing areas of blindness, unbelief, and immaturity in the hearts of sincere and genuine believers.

God uses our conflicts for his redemptive purposes as we respond to them, not only from our temporal perspective but from the eternal perspective of living for God's glory. God is still in control. As we keep our focus on God, we guard our hearts from compromise and discouragement. Timothy Lane and Paul Tripp describe this well in their book *How People Change.*

Any time we find ourselves in difficulty or trial, it is easy to think we have been forgotten or rejected by God. This is because we do not understand the present process. God is not working for our comfort and ease; he is working on our growth. At the very moment we are tempted to question his faithfulness, he is fulfilling his redemptive promises to us. After all, it's not like there are only some people who really need to change. Change is the norm for everyone, and God is always at work to complete this process in us.[2]

Faith matters. We can maintain hope for the redemption of church conflict only if we have a theology that embraces a very big and a completely sovereign, eternal God. If we do not believe Romans 8:28–29 that God is using "all things" to conform his children to the image of Christ, we will undoubtedly have a weak view of God's ability to change people. This will lead us to avoid confrontation. ("Why should I even try to talk with him? *He'll never change.*") Rather than praying, studying, and preparing wisely, we will be frozen in inaction, paralyzed by unbelief. Without a right view of God, we will respond to our church's conflicts as many Christians do—they don't even *try* to work through the conflicts. Overwhelmed with the thought of things going poorly, people being resistant, or the conflict only worsening, many Christians fail to engage. But when we see God rightly and worship him above all else, then we can have the courage to engage. When Christians remember that God uses even our weakness to reveal his strength (2 Cor. 12:9), that God is a covenant-keeping God of his Word (Gen. 9:16; 2 Sam. 23:5; Isa. 54:10; 55:3; Heb. 13:20), that God has made promises never to forsake his church (Deut. 31:6; Matt. 28:20; Heb. 13:5), then we will always have great hope, no matter how bleak our current situation may seem.

Again consider Moses, faced with the seemingly impossible task of confronting the conflict between Pharaoh and the Israelites (Exod. 7:4). Moses had doubts. Moses was weak. But God used Moses even when he was weak. And as Moses saw that God was a God of his promises, Moses grew stronger and became a great spiritual leader. We can have this same confidence in God as we are co-laborers with Christ, seeking the redemption of our church's conflicts.

Apply This to Your Church Conflict

As you reflect on your church's conflicts, we encourage you to open your Bible and read Psalm 23 with the specifics of your church conflict firmly in view. "The LORD is my shepherd, I shall not be in want. He makes me lie down in green pastures, he leads me beside quiet waters, he restores my soul. He guides me in paths of righteousness for his name's sake" (vv. 1–3).

Verses 1 through 3 not only remind us of who it is we follow in times of conflict but also how we each are called to trust his shepherding leadership—to lie down in his green pastures and to be constantly restored in the presence of his quiet waters, even in the midst of the uncertainty and anxiety of conflict. Such trusting is guided not by a blind, purposeless faith but by our certain knowledge that this path, this response to conflict, is a righteous one to be followed for the sake of his name and for his eternal glory. In other words, an eternal purpose and reason stand behind our act of faith as we trust God. Redeeming church conflict results in the growth of trust.

Verse 4, the very center of the psalm, calls us to live without fear in the midst of the "death valleys" of our lives. "Even though I walk through the valley of the shadow of death, I will fear no evil, for you are with me; your rod and your staff, they comfort me." We can live above fear (fear of man, fear of loss, fear of failure) because we know his promise to be with us is unbreakable; it has been accomplished and forever guaranteed by Christ's death on the cross (see Matt. 28:20). Knowing that we never walk alone in conflict convinces us to accept God's instruments of comfort in conflict: his rod (the instrument of spiritual authority vested in the church holding us accountable for sin) and his staff (the instrument of spiritual support we find in the fellowship of the church). Together these instruments give us assurance of our faith (comfort). Redeeming church conflict results in the growth of one's assurance of faith.

"You prepare a table before me in the presence of my enemies. You anoint my head with oil; my cup overflows. Surely goodness and love will follow me all the days of my life, and I will dwell in the house of the LORD forever" (vv. 5–6). These verses recount the covenant blessings being bestowed on those who have grown in grace, grown through this conflict by trusting God, and on those whose confidence in God is a visible by-product of a church conflict redeemed for his sake—that is, for his glory and for our spiritual maturity. These blessings include God's friendship, anointing, and everlasting protection in his presence.

Remember that this life is but a vapor (James 4:14). "A thousand years in [God's] sight are like a day that has just gone by" (Ps. 90:4). And though your church conflict may feel overwhelming and everlasting, it is not. Your real home is in eternity to come and so we learn "to number our days aright, that we may gain a heart of wisdom" (Ps. 90:12).

> Therefore we do not lose heart. Though outwardly we are wasting away, yet inwardly we are being renewed day by day. For our light and momentary troubles are achieving for us an eternal glory that far outweighs them all. So we fix our eyes not on what is seen, but on what is unseen. For what is seen is temporary, but what is unseen is eternal. (2 Corinthians 4:16–18)

Questions for Reflection

1. What are your greatest fears both for yourself and for your church at this moment? How will you keep these fears from extinguishing your hope for you and for your church's future?
2. What excuses seem most available at the present time? Are any of them legitimate? Why or why not?
3. What "assignment" has God given you in your church conflict? What steps will you take to trust God and faithfully redeem your church's present conflicts?

Recommended Resources for Further Study

Jerry Bridges, *Trusting God: Even When Life Hurts* (Colorado Springs: NavPress, 1988).

J. Ligon Duncan III, *Does Grace Grow Best in Winter?* (Phillipsburg, NJ: P&R Publishing, 2009).

R. C. Sproul, *The Holiness of God* (Wheaton: Tyndale, 1988).

4

Actions, Desires, and Beliefs

For out of the overflow of his heart his mouth speaks.

Luke 6:45

People change when they see they are responsible for what they believe about God. Life experience is no excuse for believing lies; the world and Devil don't excuse the flesh. People change when biblical truth becomes more loud and vivid than previous life experience.

David Powlison

Everything we ever say or do is the result of some kind of desire. We raise our voice at our secretary because she fails to do a task in the exact way we want. In that moment, our actions reveal our true desires—I wanted the task done more than I wanted to honor this person, even more than I wanted to love God.

Such desires show what we really believe (about the church, the gospel, ourselves, others, God, the issues in conflict). For example, how do we tend to process a verbal attack during a church conflict? It can be easy to merely feel threatened (*I'm under attack!*) and respond accordingly (run away or retaliate). But God gives us the grace to engage our thinking in a much different way so that our actual response is based on our foundational beliefs. For example, *My brother in Christ has said harsh and demeaning words to me.*

I cannot overlook them and unilaterally forgive them. I must go and speak with him so that we can work through this conflict and be reconciled. This response is probably what we really believe because we know what the Bible says about forgiveness and unity among Christians. But the questions remain: Do we connect what we *believe* with what we *do?* Or do we merely respond out of our passionate desires?

Belief and acting on belief are two different things. How we process what we are going to do is different from belief. All Christians in conflicted churches believe that Jesus is Lord, but all too often we do not live consistently with the implications of that belief. Peter's argument for consistency between what we believe and what we do is made at Acts 15:9–10: "[God] made no distinction between us and them, for he purified their hearts by faith. Now then, why do you try to test God by putting on the necks of the disciples a yoke that neither we nor our fathers have been able to bear?"

Just as Peter argued for consistency, let's consider the consistency of our beliefs and actions as we face conflict. Doing this shows what we really believe, not just what we profess to believe. Doing this reveals what we truly desire (our heart motivations). When biblical knowledge and biblical practice align, church conflicts are avoided or redeemed. But at the root of all destructive church conflicts, something has gone askew with our thinking, believing, and our desires (our heart motivations).

Presenting Issues

Frequently what has gone askew is seen in how the issues of conflict are presented. Usually they are stated in terms of *presenting issues*—the obvious problems to be solved or points of disagreement. ("The problem is the pastor/worship style/lack of funding for women's ministry/some other issue.")

Whenever we have been asked to help a conflicted church, we first hear about the *presenting issues*—the apparent reasons for the church being in conflict. Each church is unique and the conflicts of each church are unique, but often the presenting issues can be generally categorized, as Ken Sande has recognized:

1. Internal conflicts (indecision, substance abuse, bitterness)
2. Material conflicts (Should we adopt a new curriculum? What color should the pew cushions be?)
3. Value and belief conflicts (doctrine, prioritizing church ministries, abortion)
4. Relationship conflicts (personal offenses, unforgiveness, divorce)
5. Information conflicts (selective release of information, misrepresentation)
6. System conflicts (confusion regarding responsibilities or chain of command)[1]

Most church conflicts are a combination of multiple categories of presenting issues. Here are a few examples.

- A pastor has an internal struggle with pornography. This leads to relational conflicts in his family. He tries to hide his personal sins and avoid the deterioration in his home life by working long hours and demanding more and more from his staff. This leads to more relational conflicts and ultimately to a material conflict over whether the pastor should be retained or let go.
- Two women disagree over which Bible study should be used in the summer women's program. Initially this was just a simple conflict over a material question, but now the women are personally conflicted. Their estrangement is growing, and other women are feeling pressured to take sides because only selective information is being shared, so uncharitable and inaccurate perspectives on the situation abound.
- The deacons make a decision to spend a large sum of money. They believe that they have the authority to make this decision, but some people disagree. Rather than quietly and gently talking with the deacons about their concerns, some passionate (and angry) people schedule a formal meeting to publicly rebuke and reprove the deacons. Many of the deacons are so offended that they immediately resign and threaten to remove their families from the church. The complaining group feels bad about this but they still believe they are right.

As you consider your church's conflicts, it may be helpful to try to identify the issues in the form of questions to be answered. This is what we as mediators do whenever we are helping people in conflict. Then these questions help make up the working agenda (as issues) covering all of the matters to be addressed. For example, your church conflict might have issue statements something like these:

- Should the pastor be released from his call? If so, why?
- Which Bible study should the summer women's program use?
- Was it appropriate for the deacons to spend such a large sum of money?

Presenting issues like these are what mediators call *material* or *substantive* issues. They are usually concrete questions that can be answered with concrete responses. Material issues can also be negotiated, whereas *personal* (also called *relational*) issues are less concrete; they can be hard to describe and define. In most cases personal issues have emotional overtones and, unlike material issues, are *not* resolved through negotiation but through repentance, confession, and forgiveness.

Personal issues should be addressed by asking questions like the following:

- How can the pastor best be helped to overcome his internal struggle with pornography? And how can the pastor's marriage, parenting, and staff relationships be restored?
- What will it take for the two women to be personally reconciled to each other? What steps do they need to take to reconcile the relationships in the church that have become conflicted in the wake of their dispute?
- How can concerned families have a restored relationship with the deacons? How can the deacons be helped to forgive the people who organized the offending meeting?

It is time-consuming and difficult to identify and categorize all of the material and personal presenting issues, but it is necessary. The goal is to get to the point where each person involved in the church conflict can say, "If we deal with these issues, our church conflicts will be resolved."

Once the issues are listed, they should be ranked by priority and addressed in order of importance because, even in an extensive church intervention process, it may be impossible to address every issue. This is particularly true because, as we begin to work through the issues, new issues almost always arise, which is to be expected. When this happens, we simply add the additional issues to the agenda, prioritize them, and continue working. The hope is that, if we can make a little progress on the big issues, the other sub-issues can be resolved through less formal means; and some issues will simply be eliminated as certain solutions are embraced and implemented.

Heart Motivations

After we have the issues listed, it's time to state the various conflicted *positions*—for example, the pastor should be removed vs. the pastor should *not* be removed—and begin to drill down to the heart motivations underlying the various positions.

A heart motivation (or interest) is defined as the primary reason a person favors one position over another. It reflects *desire* and can be based on a fear of loss, an overwhelming passion for a gain, or an even more selfish motive to satisfy an ingrained idol. Moving to heart motivations is the only way we can move away from simple power bargaining over positions. As we understand the reasons various people are clinging to various positions, we can begin to see more clearly the exclusive interests and the shared interests that may be held by the opposing parties. The exclusive interests are the interests that are actually in conflict—one interest *excludes* the other interest. The shared interests provide strategic points for potential agreement even among conflicted people—these interests agree. This process of identifying underlying interests will reveal the real desires that are driving the conflicts.

It is difficult to move from presenting issues to heart motivations, but it is necessary. As we do so, we will see that rarely will anyone present his or her position as being purely arbitrary or capricious; the pull of self-justification and self-righteousness is simply too strong. Almost always people try to justify the rightness of their desired outcome. Those perpetuating conflict in the church will frequently do so by presenting an issue that makes them look spiritual and righteous. The only way to accurately evaluate heart motivations is to compare the evidence of those motivations (words, attitudes, countenance, and so on) with the propositional truth of Holy Scripture. The fixed standard of the Bible will help determine which heart motivations are legitimate (God-honoring and comporting with God's standards) and which are illegitimate (sinful, selfish, lacking in faith and a love for God and neighbor).

Understanding the heart's motives helps to reveal not only *what* people do but also *why* they do what they do in conflict. Knowing what is motivating people in conflict allows you to adjust your expectations and minister more effectively and compassionately to their fears while insightfully addressing their passions. Jesus illustrates this in Luke 12:13–21.

> Someone in the crowd said to him, "Teacher, tell my brother to divide the inheritance with me."
>
> Jesus replied, "Man, who appointed me a judge or an arbiter between you?" Then he said to them, "Watch out! Be on your guard against all kinds of greed; a man's life does not consist in the abundance of his possessions." (vv. 13–15)

Jesus sees past the *presenting issue*—how to divide the inheritance (an apparently reasonable request)—to the *real issue*—a greedy heart. Whenever we begin to address church conflicts, we too must strive to discern the real issues underlying the presenting issues. Determining the presenting issues is only the first step. We must consider not only *what* people want but *why* they want it if we are to understand the motivations of the heart.

James 4:1–4 explains that our conflicts reveal underlying heart issues.

> What causes fights and quarrels among you? Don't they come from your desires that battle within you? You want something but don't get it. You kill and covet, but you cannot have what you want. You quarrel and fight. You do not have, because you do not ask God. When you

why things don't "just go away"

ask, you do not receive, because you ask with wrong motives, that you may spend what you get on your pleasures.

You adulterous people, don't you know that friendship with the world is hatred toward God?

Scripture places the cause of quarrels and fights at the doorstep of our heart's unmet desires, which are rooted in our selfish passions. We want what we want, and if we don't get what we want, we do things that cause further conflict. Caught up in our desires, we become blind in the depth of our selfish passions. James's question is a rhetorical weapon he uses to diagnose our self-centeredness, and God calls us an "adulterous people" because we are self-centered rather than God-centered.

By giving our time, attention, emotions, money, and love to our desires, we are living as enemies of God. When we fight, quarrel, hate, and devour one another in the church, our loyalty is to our desires and passions, not to God. Presenting issues and the positions (desired outcomes) favored by opponents may reveal what is wrong with our hearts.

Our adultery is revealed when we spend time discerning the reasons we want what we want. In church conflict we see adultery revealed as people press for *their* agenda without a thought given to considering humbly the needs of others. But when we demonstrate humility and prayerfully strive to maintain and guard unity in the church, we are living as faithful children. And as Paul makes clear in Philippians 2:2, unity in the body of Christ is at the core of God's purpose and mission for the church.

It is God's central agenda that we all have his agenda. There should be no time for fighting among ourselves in the church over any other agenda. Being faithful to God's agenda for the church is the exact opposite of being an adulterous people. When we, as God's eternal children inhabiting his church, contribute to the prevention and redemption of destructive conflicts in his church, then we are turning away from our spiritual adultery, from our agendas, and adopting his agenda. This changes every aspect of how we deal with conflicts in the church.

Unity as Christians becomes our task when we face conflict. Unity becomes our common priority because we discover our priorities in what God says are his priorities. Unity becomes a demonstration of our faithfulness. And God's priority for unity between his eternal children is one of his highest (see Rom. 14:19; Eph. 4:3; Heb. 12:14). Also God warns us, "If you keep on biting and devouring each other, watch out or you will be destroyed by each other" (Gal. 5:15). The unchecked end of our unbridled passions and desires is consumption. That is clearly not God's intention for his church, the church he calls "the Bride" for his returning Son.

Rather than answering the question, What causes church conflict? by addressing only presenting issues, we must realize that those issues are merely the symptoms of the fact that too many of God's people simply don't understand, and subsequently do not do, the faithful work of building God's church. We don't know what it means to be a disciple of Christ, so we don't know what it means to be a faithful church member. We don't know what God's intention for the church is, so we can't find unity with others around a common intention. We don't appreciate what it means to have been called to unity in Christ and, therefore, we don't do everything possible to be in unity with one another.

In subsequent chapters, we address what leaders should be doing to help people understand God's plan for the church in bringing about change to hearts that have been hardened by conflict. For truly what people don't know leads to people not doing, or worse, doing things that are antithetical to building God's church. Ultimately our words and actions reflect what is in our hearts (see Matt. 12:34–37). Our call is to apply our knowledge of God faithfully through consistent acts as we confront the challenges of conflict. Without the knowledge that leads to heart change, we cannot begin to act with consistency and appreciate what God is really up to. And in church conflict God is up to a lot!

Two Mini Case Studies

I (Dave) led an intervention team in a church that had huge conflicts between two groups: the senior pastor and elders (who were united) versus younger members of the congregation. At some point during the mediation process, my co-mediator and I had everyone stop and read 2 Timothy 2:22–26.

> Flee the evil desires of youth, and pursue righteousness, faith, love and peace, along with those who call on the Lord out of a pure heart. Don't have anything to do with foolish and stupid arguments, because you know they produce quarrels. And the Lord's servant must not quarrel; instead, he must be kind to everyone, able to teach, not resentful. Those who oppose him he must gently instruct, in the hope that God will grant them repentance leading them to a knowledge of the truth, and that they will come to their senses and escape from the trap of the devil, who has taken them captive to do his will.

As the mediation progressed, we noticed that something was going on with the senior pastor; he was becoming more and more agitated. So we called for a private meeting with the pastor and we asked him what was happening. At first, he could not even respond to us. He was so convicted by the Word of God that it was almost as if we could see him changing right before our eyes. It was quite dramatic. He said that he saw clearly now that the issues being fought over were not the issues at all. The real problem was that he was a foolish man involved in a foolish argument driven by his selfish desires that had produced a quarrel in the church and *he* was the threat to unity. He was devastated as he saw his failures as the spiritual leader; he was just as caught up in the conflict as anybody; he was not showing a different attitude of humility; he was not leading with a servant's heart. Just like the elders, he was fighting back, proudly justifying what they had done. He was completely failing to shepherd and lead the other members of his flock. And God was convicting him that he needed to repent, to change, and to demonstrate his repentance by his deeds.

He was so convicted that his heart motivations were sinful, he said he could not in good conscience continue with the mediation because he had to go and meet with the other side privately, right away. He wanted to confess to them that he had gotten caught up in the controversy and had failed to minister to them. Rather than serving and protecting and leading them as their pastor, he had been treating them as enemies. In response to the pastor's confession, the other side was surprised and suspicious but they grudgingly accepted his confession. Even the elders were confused as the pastor stepped away from their side and insisted on being apart from the controversy so that he could minister to everyone in his flock.

God's Word softened his heart and changed his entire response to the conflict. In that moment, he was an instrument in Christ's hands, co-laboring with him to redeem the church's conflict. Seeing his heart motivations in light of God's truth changed his entire perspective. Even though some of the members refused to accept his confession and even resigned their membership, he still redeemed the conflict. God's Word did the hard work; we were simply there to facilitate the process by gently holding forth the Scripture and helping the parties see their underlying heart motivations in light of God's Word.

In contrast to that example, we both worked with a young pastor who knew Scripture inside and out but who stubbornly refused to see the heart motivations that were ruling his life in contradiction to God's Word. As mediators who were outside of the conflict, we saw it clearly. His fellow church leaders and many laypeople in his congregation saw it. (He was even subsequently brought up on formal charges by his denominational leaders.) But even in light of overwhelming evidence and the testimony of people who were devoted to him and loved him as a brother and a shepherd, he adamantly clung to his desires. His heart motivations trumped every other consideration. He lost all spiritual objectivity and evidenced a complete lack of wisdom and discernment; and as far as we know, to date, he has never repented. Still, his fellow church leaders are comforted in knowing that they were faithful to God and to their responsibilities to love and lead this young man. They redeemed the conflict, even though this young man, sadly, never did.

Apply This to Your Church Conflict

As ⁓ eflect on how Jesus addressed the rich man in Luke 12:18–21, ow the Lord exposed the layers of rationalization and re- ₂ real nature of the man's heart. Rather than stewarding ⁓ions so that he could be rich toward God, the man was clinging to his possessions more than he was clinging to God. Jesus revealed reality, which is apparent only through the lens of his eternal perspective, not that of a selfish heart. True discernment comes when we are grafted into God's ultimate purposes, and that will never happen when confronting merely the presenting issues. Even if the process is honorable and fair, it will not bring real peace or ultimately resolve the conflict unless it flushes out the true causes of conflict, and then brings the gospel to bear.

As you think about what you believe and what desires are ruling your heart in your church conflict, remember that often the evil in our desires is not in what we want but in the fact that we want it too much. If we are overwhelmed by a passion for something other than Christ—even something good—we will begin to be ruled by that passion. We will forget why we are Christians, what the purpose of our church is, and that our real life is in eternity to come. To redeem our church's conflict, we are called to be ruled by a passion for Christ, for the glory of his fame.

Questions for Reflection

1. Think about the things that excite you in life. What really motivates you? What makes you happy? What are you living for? Now consider: What does the Bible say should be your true delight?
2. Considering your unique personality, gifts, and life experiences, how have you sought intentionally to connect what you believe as a Christian with how you act?
3. How would others describe what you want most out of your church's present conflicts? Do you believe those perceptions would accurately reflect what you believe most deeply as a Christian? Why or why not?
4. What are the most significant presenting issues of your church's conflicts? Do you think these are the real issues or are there other underlying heart motivations involved in the conflict? If so, what are they? Will addressing these underlying heart motivations get to the most critical aspects of the conflict? Why or why not?

Recommended Resources for Further Study

Carolyn Custis James, *When Life and Beliefs Collide: How Knowing God Makes a Difference* (Grand Rapids: Zondervan, 2001).

John Piper, *Think: The Life of the Mind and the Love of God* (Wheaton: Crossway, 2010).

Paul David Tripp, *A Quest for More: Living for Something Bigger than You* (Greensboro, NC: New Growth Press, 2007).

Section 2

Discernment

A rich man may be wise in his own eyes, but a poor man who has discernment sees through him.

Proverbs 28:11

One of the most subtle burdens God ever puts on us as saints is this burden of discernment concerning other souls. He reveals things in order that we may take the burden of these souls before Him and form the mind of Christ about them. It is not that we bring God into touch with our minds, but that we rouse ourselves until God is able to convey His mind to us about the one for whom we intercede.

Oswald Chambers

Even with a renewed perspective, the members of LCC still had much discussion and debate ahead of them if they were going to be discerning and truly redeem their church's conflicts. This was particularly true because the mediation team had quickly helped them see that their own members did not understand what the conflicts were, let alone what was causing them. Initially they listed more than twenty different conflicts and potential causes, so they had no idea which conflicts to address first. They were overwhelmed.

We helped them move forward by teaching them how to ask best (not just right) questions and how to listen well. Focusing on positions and interests, here are examples of problem identification:

1. Before any material issues were addressed, the church's leaders and members had to repent of spiritual blindness regarding how they had forgotten God's interests in their church's conflicts. As they answered the question, How is God being affected by the conflicts we have identified? they quickly saw that they had been prioritizing their interests ahead of his. Their corporate sin painfully began to lead them not only to repentance before God but also to repentance and confession toward one another. They were eager to be right with God and reconciled personally.
2. Rather than asking which governance structure was better (elder-led or congregational), the members and leaders asked why they thought one governance structure was better than the other. This led to meaningful discussions about fear of the loss of control and fear of not being able to lead the church well. And once the heart of the question was on the table, the solution (trust in God!) was clear and unanimous. It also led them to make a wise and unified decision regarding the governance structure they would use going forward.
3. They also asked why one group wanted a traditional worship service and improvements to the existing building and why the other group wanted a more modern service and a gymnasium built.

And then we helped them listen to one another, for we had seen early on that both groups truly believed that their positions were the best way to glorify God and love their neighbors. But it wasn't enough for us to see this as mediators; the members and leaders needed to have that aha experience themselves. Once they did, they were ready to move on to biblical solutions, but only because their leaders were ready to lead and members were ready to follow.

A normal response to church conflict is simply to be overwhelmed. Conflict between just two people can be a source of anxiety and fear and be hard to work through. Any kind of organizational conflict brings a greater level of complication. And when issues of theology and polity are added to the group dynamic, the challenges increase exponentially. It may seem impossible even to identify the problems, let alone begin to discuss and evaluate possible solutions. But it is not impossible. It is complicated and it requires prayerful effort, but it is possible to be discerning and wise even in church conflict.

As Peter demonstrates in Acts 15, discernment requires *careful discussion*:

> Then some of the believers who belonged to the party of the Pharisees stood up and said, "The Gentiles must be circumcised and required to obey the law of Moses."
>
> The apostles and elders met to consider this question. After much discussion, Peter got up and addressed them. (Acts 15:5–7)

The problem is, when a church is severely conflicted, communication breaks down. Gentle, wise, and productive discussion is not usually the norm. Lifetime friends are shocked to find themselves as opponents because they are consumed by the pull and force of competing groups. Virtual strangers become intimate allies as members who have remained on the church roster for years without any meaningful participation suddenly show up to defend their convictions regarding their church. Someone dusts off the *Book of Church Order* or other corporate documents for the first time in decades—not to seek wisdom and help but to defeat a perceived enemy and force through a desired outcome.

It takes prayer, humility, faith, and great skill to facilitate thorough and open discussion between Christians in conflict. It also requires wisdom to discern the best (not just the right) questions that need to be asked. One of the reasons church conflict explodes to the point of destroying a church is that individual members and leaders, and the corporate entity as a body, have long-standing patterns of responding to conflict by instinctively trying to answer immediate, demanding questions before they have even considered what the best questions should be. As mentioned in the previous chapter, this is called addressing presenting issues. For Christian mediators, it is never enough to address only the presenting issues; heart motivations must also be considered. It is understandable that many people get stuck dealing only with apparent issues—those issues may now be obvious as people are incessant in demanding that their issues receive quick attention. But real wisdom, true discernment, goes far beyond the facilitating-good-communication stage that any one of a thousand books on listening skills and asking good questions can offer.

Careful discussion and asking the best questions will help everyone involved navigate the group dynamics and be better equipped to listen to self, others, and God. When seeking to redeem church conflicts, the goal of any discussion is not merely to communicate in such a way that the other side understands our perspectives and convictions. This is important but it is not of first importance. To redeem your church's conflict, the goal of any discussion you have ought to be the aha moment when you understand clearly what your heart motivations are and what God calls you to do and say in order to live according to his Word; then you conform your attitudes, words, and actions to God's requirements. Yes, you may also have an opportunity to help others do the same, but regardless of their responses, you can grow in your sanctification.

We can be wise—discerning—according to the standard given in James 3:13–18.

> Who is wise and understanding among you? Let him show it by his good life, by deeds done in the humility that comes from wisdom. But if you harbor bitter envy and selfish ambition in your hearts, do not boast about it or deny the truth. Such "wisdom" does not come down from heaven but is earthly, unspiritual, of the devil. For where you have envy and selfish ambition, there you find disorder and every evil practice.
>
> But the wisdom that comes from heaven is first of all pure; then peace-loving, considerate, submissive, full of mercy and good fruit, impartial and sincere. Peacemakers who sow in peace raise a harvest of righteousness.

I (Dave) worked with the leaders of a Christian school who had completely bought into a certain strategy for educating children. When the strategy came under question by some parents and affiliated church leaders, the school leadership became incensed. Two other mediators and I were tasked with facilitating the discussion between the school leaders and the parents/church leaders. To do so, I began by asking the school leaders to bring their manuals for the education program. They all did as I requested, and I saw that their manuals were well-used, dog-eared, filled with Post-it notes and scribbles. So I asked them to turn to the section in their manuals that dealt with how to glorify God and love neighbor in the education of children. They all started flipping pages, looking in the index, talking among themselves; but ultimately they had to admit that there was nothing in there about those topics.

Of course, I knew this was true before the meeting because I had looked through the manual and I had seen its huge deficiencies for a Christian school. That's how I knew to ask the "best question" for that specific group. If I had just said to them, "This system has huge deficiencies," they would have either argued with me or dismissed me out of hand. By facilitating their aha moment, their conviction and discovery, I helped them experience the pain and joy of self-discovery.

Careful, facilitated discussion and the asking of best questions help people come to their own discovery about what they are really believing, saying, and doing. Questions provoke heart engagement regarding core beliefs and motivations, whereas declarative statements invite defensiveness, blame shifting, and excuse making. Rather than jumping to a premature conclusion or solution, asking the best questions helps us have clearer insight and discernment to more accurately mine the depths of Scripture and test whether we are living in line with God's Word. Questions are one way that we train ourselves to "distinguish good from evil" (Heb. 5:14). The best news about discernment is that it can come only by the power of the Holy Spirit as God's living and active Word pierces even the hardest hearts and removes the scales of blindness from our eyes. Therefore, true discernment and God-honoring discussion will bring glory to God and demonstrate love for neighbor because they can come only by grace through faith in Christ.

5

Much Discussion and Debate

A fool finds no pleasure in understanding but delights in airing his own opinions.

Proverbs 18:2

We owe our opponents to deal with them in such a way they may sense that we have a real interest in them as persons, that we are not simply trying to win an argument or show how smart we are, but that we are deeply interested in them—and are eager to learn from them as well as to help them.

Roger Nicole

Discussion was a key dynamic of the work of the apostles and elders as they met in Jerusalem to redeem the early church's first major conflict. Verse 7 of Acts 15 says, "After much discussion." What was that discussion like? We know the issue—must the Gentiles be circumcised to be saved? That is, of course, only a narrow statement of the issue, as those advocating that view (the Judaizers) really desired that all of the Old Testament's rules and laws be practiced by Christians for them to truly be considered a part of God's family (see v. 5, "to obey the law of Moses"). Paul knew he must oppose the Judaizers because forcing Gentiles to be circumcised might lead them to think that salvation must be earned, and that would hinder the work of the gospel. Of course, it was also not true! We know Paul was vehemently opposed to this view.

Did Paul use strong language during the discussion at Jerusalem? We know the whole assembly was present as this discussion took place (v. 12). We don't know what Paul said exactly other than that he "reported everything God had done through them" (v. 4), and spoke "about the miraculous signs and wonders God had done among the Gentiles through them [Paul and Barnabas]" (v. 12). We don't know the tone Paul took with the Judaizers during this discussion but we do know that his opposition to them was "sharp" (v. 2), because he firmly held to what he believed the gospel message was, recorded in Galatians 2:15–16:

> We who are Jews by birth and not "Gentile sinners" know that a man is not justified by observing the law, but by faith in Jesus Christ. So we, too, have put our faith in Christ Jesus that we may be justified by faith in Christ and not by observing the law, because by observing the law no one will be justified.

Apparently Paul left it to Peter and James to make the convincing arguments that the Gentiles, too, had the Holy Spirit (Acts 15:8), that God had "purified their hearts by faith" (v. 9), and that the words of the prophets were in accord with what Peter had said (vv. 15–18). Then James set forth his judgment that the Gentiles should not have barriers erected that would make it more difficult for them to turn to God (v. 19). Paul was, undoubtedly, delighted by James's statement, but the text does not go into any further revelation about that other than to say "It seemed good to the Holy Spirit and to us . . ." (v. 28), affirming that a decision that was the voice of the majority had been reached.

In the church today we have people like the Judaizers who call themselves "Christian" but advocate, just as the Judaizers did, a gospel weighed down with additions that do not reflect God's agenda for the church. Church conflicts are resolved and redeemed for God's glory and the spiritual growth of his people as the basics of the gospel are recaptured and thrust to the forefront. *We are unaware of any church that has successfully resolved its churchwide conflicts without first going back to the basics of what the gospel message is, its implications for faith and life, and God's statement of purpose and mission for his church*—just as that first church council at Jerusalem had to do! When Christians are united around God's purpose and mission for the church, all other matters fade away. But until meaningful discussion can bring everyone to that perspective, it is unlikely that progress to redeem conflict can be made. All too often people stop communicating and the discussions that need to take place never do.

The purpose of discussion when seeking peace is to regain God's perspective for the church. To accomplish this with grace means remembering many things about communication in the church: what questions are the best questions, how do we control our tongue so that we speak "truth in love" (Eph. 4:15) and not merely truth as we perceive it in a voice of anger, and how can we serve God by fulfilling his call for our unity (Phil. 2:2)?

Redemptive Discussion in Conflicted Churches

Once conflicted parties have done the hard work of discerning the issues, positions, and interests (underlying heart motivations) in a church's conflict and are continuing to fix their hearts on a Christ-centered, eternal perspective, they are ready to redeem their discussions. Ephesians provides the standard for our speech:

> Do not let any unwholesome talk come out of your mouths, but only what is helpful for building others up according to their needs, that it may benefit those who listen. And do not grieve the Holy Spirit of God, with whom you were sealed for the day of redemption. Get rid of all bitterness, rage and anger, brawling and slander, along with every form of malice. (Ephesians 4:29–31)

We must do the following to meet this biblical standard:

- Remember that conflicted conversations are usually adrenaline-producing and full of strong emotions. Prepare in advance by recognizing where temptations will be and have a plan for responding in edifying, gracious ways. Prayer will be a key part of this step as will the discipline to ask of every statement you are tempted to make: Does this meet the Ephesians 4:29 standards for speech? Is it edifying? Does it communicate grace to the hearer? (If not, then you should not say it.)

- Do not expect perfection from yourself or others. Conversations almost always have miscommunications and misunderstandings; how much more so when relationships are strained and emotions are raw. Engage anyway. Have the conversation. Meditate on Romans 12 and then talk and listen to those on opposing sides.

- To actually communicate with others in a church conflict, all must listen until you are able to define all of the terms being used. (This will ensure that you understand one another.) And you should listen until you can outline an accurate understanding of all perspectives and convictions. If you can state back to others what they are saying and they agree that you understand them, then you can be confident that you are listening effectively and having a redemptive conversation.

- Look for common positions and interests and emphasize any agreements you have with your opponent. Much trust can be built even by saying something as simple as "We still have much disagreement, but I agree with you about . . ."

- Be flexible and charitable. Give to your opponents the same degree of grace and charitable presumption that you want them to give to you. Remember that you are one in Christ, even as you differ on important topics in your church conflict. Remembering this truth will help you not to slander. The Greek word *diabolos* (translated "slanderer") is used thirty-four times in the Bible as a title for Satan. We act like Satan when we falsely accuse—slander—others. "Brothers, do not slander one another" (James 4:11).

As we consider all of the discussions and debates we are engaged in related to church conflict, we are reminded of the seriousness of this issue. "If anyone considers himself religious and yet does not keep a tight rein on his tongue, he deceives himself and his religion is worthless" (James 1:26). "He who guards his lips guards his life, but he who speaks rashly will come to ruin" (Prov. 13:3).

Talk That Changes Us

Something we may never have asked ourselves regarding church conflict is, *What is the* purpose *of my talking?* Most of us just talk. We are not intentional or purposeful and sometimes we don't even listen to ourselves. But *redemptive talk* has a self-reflective element to it. We don't just talk so the other person hears us; we talk so we can understand ourselves and better conform our thinking, believing, speaking, and acting to Holy Scripture.

Through redemptive speech, we can understand our own positions on the various issues and see with greater clarity the desires and attitudes that underlie these positions. We recognize where we are prone to exaggerate, use loaded vocabulary, or even tell a little white lie. Because of our commitment to God and the standards he has established in his Word, we are called to repent of any talk that is not honest and edifying. Our goal is to live up to the standard set in 1 Peter 2 and 3:

> Live such good lives among the pagans that, though they accuse you of doing wrong, they may see your good deeds and glorify God on the day he visits us. . . . For it is God's will that by doing good you should silence the ignorant talk of foolish men. . . . But do this with gentleness and respect, keeping a clear conscience, so that those who speak maliciously against your good behavior in Christ may be ashamed of their slander. (1 Peter 2:12, 15; 3:15–16)

Since we are called to live in accordance with such a standard before "pagans" and "foolish men," how much more so are we called to live in this way among our siblings in Christ in the church. As Ken Sande so aptly states in *The Peacemaker*:

> The more intense a dispute becomes, the more important it is to control your tongue (Rom. 12:14). When you are involved in prolonged conflict, you may be sorely tempted to indulge in gossip, slander, and reckless words, especially if your opponent is saying critical things about you. But if you react with harsh words or gossip, you will only make matters worse. Even if your opponent speaks maliciously against you or to you, do not respond in kind. Instead, make every effort to breathe grace by saying only what is both true

and helpful, speaking well of your opponent whenever possible, and using kind and gracious language. As Peter wrote, "Do not repay evil with evil or insult with insult, but with blessing, because to this you were called so that you may inherit a blessing" (1 Peter 3:9; cf. 1 Cor. 4:12–13).[1]

A Mini Case Study

I (Dave) first came into contact with Pastor Carl and his wife, Rita, after their church had hired me to lead a team of mediators in a church intervention. I started receiving calls from church members even before we had solicited initial information concerning the conflict. The first call was from Rita.

Rita's Story

Rita and Carl had been married for twenty years. After Carl finished seminary, they had planned to be foreign missionaries. Rita had dreamed of marrying a missionary and living abroad as a part of her husband's missionary team. But a complicated pregnancy with twin boys had prevented that and Carl took a position instead as an associate pastor near their parents. After five years as an associate, a senior pastorate position became available at a nice, financially stable church in the suburbs of a major Midwestern city. Carl's experience and training earned him this new position, and the first few years went pretty well.

Ten years passed. Now the boys were juniors in high school, excited about their coming senior year, after which they would attend the nearby state university with plans to live at home for the first couple of years. Carl and Rita had purchased a beautiful home where they could entertain church guests and play a visible role in the social life of the church and the community. Life had been great until recently.

Confusion and conflict began to surface when the elder board passed a resolution temporarily suspending her husband from his job while additional inquiries were made concerning the effectiveness of his ministry and whether he should remain in his position. Rita's world was crashing; she could not understand how the elders could do such a thing after all the hard work Carl and she had poured into the church, their life's work. All of Rita's closest friends were in the church and they had called her with difficult questions after the elders had announced the action. She was very upset by these calls, which had embarrassed her and for which she didn't have any real answers. She was terrified for the family and their plans for the boys. And what if she had to move away from her beautiful home? That would just be too much!

Carl's Story, as Related by Rita

The elders had not explained why Carl was being temporarily suspended. They had said only that they felt the time was right for some significant changes to be made at the church. When Rita pressed Carl about what was really going on, she was surprised to hear how difficult his relationship with the chairman of the elders, George, had become and how they had clashed at elder meetings. Carl had withheld this information from Rita because he did not want to upset the close relationship that Rita had with George's wife. Carl further related that he felt, while his preaching was well received, his leadership of a strong elder board was failing. The men serving as elders were powerful men, and Carl admitted to Rita that he felt out of his league trying to work with them. Carl considered his suspension as an effort of the elders to position the church to compete with two megachurches in the area that had grown quickly. Carl's confidence was low and his initial resolve to stay engaged in the life of the church was weakening. Rita told me she could not accept her husband's attitude and had recently been encouraging him to step up and regain control of the situation.

Rita's Plea

Rita's first question to me was about her husband. "What should he do to prepare for the intervention process to be in the best position to take an appeal to the denomination if things don't work out?" I didn't answer that question. Rather, I first had to take a moment to think about what the best questions would be to draw Rita away from the temporal aspects of this conflict toward a new perspective, an eternal one.

I asked her to first think about what she thought she should be doing to minister to Carl. She paused and, before she could answer, I suggested we pray together. Over the phone I led Rita in a prayer for her to trust that God was not surprised by anything that was going on, that he was sovereign over even these actions that seemed so unfair from our worldly perspective, and that she and her husband had been given this assignment from God. Their task was to discern God's reasons for giving them this specific opportunity to demonstrate their faith and trust in him. I prayed that whatever happened she and Carl and their sons together would know that they could never be separated from God's love and that they could rest assured that God was with them and that he was allowing them now to show their love, devotion, and loyalty to and for him in difficult times, just as other Christians had been given that same opportunity in countless ages past. Then I prayed that she and Carl would not be alone as they faced each day and did each next thing remembering that God's only requirement for them was faithful obedience and to trust him with the results.

Rita had begun to cry during the prayer. When I finished, and she had also said amen, I asked her if I could read a passage of Scripture to her. She said, "Of course." The passage I read was Hebrews 11:1–16. As I started with "Now faith is being sure of what we hope for and certain of what we do not see" (v. 1) and finished with the words of verse 16: "Therefore God is not ashamed to be called their God, for he has prepared a city for them," Rita again began to cry.

After a moment, allowing her to regain her composure, I asked her what she thought God might be calling her to do under these difficult circumstances. She said, and I will never forget this, "to demonstrate faith just as those ancient people did." Then I said, "Rita, you are going to be just fine. Let's meet together as soon as I arrive with the Peacemaker team to further discuss what that demonstration of your faith will look like. In the meantime, will you promise me to sit down with your husband and read with him Hebrews 11, 12, and 13, and pray with him for application of those chapters to you both at this time? She said she would.

The Rest of the Story

While the intervention process proceeded redemptively because fruitful discussions opened church members' hearts to hear God's Word, Carl and Rita decided to leave the church anyway. They sold their home and took a senior pastor position in a church on the West Coast. They now have a very promising ministry in a small rural church where they have never been happier. Yes, it took much discussion to discern and work through the many issues. But at the end of the day, Carl and Rita learned much about themselves through the extended debate that had occurred. They were drawn to keep their perspective fixed on eternity. They did not cling to idols. They rejoiced in the Lord and they trusted him with their lives, even during intense suffering and times of great uncertainty.

Apply This to Your Church Conflict

As you consider the discussions surrounding your church's conflict, consider carefully how the Lord is calling you to be edifying in your speech and to demonstrate your faith in God by your careful, respectful discourse. Philippians 4 provides a wonderful structure for your conversations:

> Rejoice in the Lord always. I will say it again: Rejoice! Let your gentleness be evident to all. The Lord is near. Do not be anxious about anything, but in everything, by prayer and petition, with thanksgiving, present your requests to God. And the peace of God, which transcends all understanding, will guard your hearts and your minds in Christ Jesus.
> Finally, brothers, whatever is true, whatever is noble, whatever is right, whatever is pure, whatever is lovely, whatever is admirable— if anything is excellent or praiseworthy—think about such things. Whatever you have learned or received or heard from me, or seen in me—put it into practice. And the God of peace will be with you. (Philippians 4:4–9)

We saw a beautiful example of such redemptive discussion and debate during one conflicted church intervention on which we both served. It was toward the end of the intervention and, together with our teammates, we had spent hours helping church leaders clarify the issues in the conflict. Talk about *much* discussion and debate! There were so many complex issues that we actually had to assign members of our mediation team to work with leader sub-groups simply to help them consolidate and prioritize all of the issues. It was extremely hard work and we were humbled by their prayerful, diligent effort.

It paid off. The careful, facilitated discussions helped the leaders see that actually they had many common interests. The leaders also saw that in their zeal to fight over various issues, they had failed to serve their sheep. So the next Sunday, the leaders stood before the congregation and asked for forgiveness for throwing their beloved people into conflict by how they, their leaders, had responded. Their humility, hard work, and willingness to own up to their contributions to the problems went a long way toward helping the entire church redeem their conflicts. It took months for bylaws, policies, and practices to be changed, but the start of it all was a commitment to stay the course, not give up, and do the hard work of engaging in much discussion and debate.

Questions for Reflection

1. Are the conflicts your church presently faces just matters of differences of opinion and/or preferences? Or are there clear sin issues involved?

2. Meditate on the words of Ephesians 4:29–31. What words have you spoken that haven't lived up to God's standard for Christian speech? Do you need to go to someone and confess your failure?

3. In your opinion, what question or comment to Rita (Pastor Carl's wife) struck you as most significant? Why? Could you use a similar question or comment to begin a process of heart change with someone stuck in conflict?

Recommended Resources for Further Study

Mike Emlet, *CrossTalk: Where Life and Scripture Meet* (Greensboro, NC: New Growth Press, 2009).

John Piper and Justin Taylor, *The Power of Words and the Wonder of God* (Wheaton: Crossway, 2008).

Paul David Tripp, *War of Words: Getting to the Heart of Your Communication Struggles* (Phillipsburg, NJ: P&R Publishing, 2000).

6

....

Asking Best (Not Just Right) Questions

The purposes of a man's heart are deep waters, but a man of understanding draws them out.

Proverbs 20:5

Insightful people are insightful not because they have the right answers
but because they have asked the right questions. If you do not ask the
right questions, you will never get to the right answers.

Paul David Tripp

Consider your specific church conflict. What are both the right
and the best questions to ask about it? Can you take the time
to really figure out what this conflict is all about, what is really
going on? Frequently people don't have a good, clear grasp of what
it is they are really fighting about. If they were to ask the best questions, they would be able to explore options that would get them
to the best answers. But usually people are all over the place. Not
so with the apostle Peter in Acts 15. He could have asked any one
of a hundred *good* questions, but instead he asks the *best* question:
"Now then, why do you try to test God by putting on the necks of
the disciples a yoke that neither we nor our fathers have been able
to bear?" (Acts 15:10).

This question goes right to the heart of the issue by engaging the
Judaizers and the other apostles as well. It demonstrates knowledge

of the issues, positions, and interests in the conflict, and it shows true discernment—discernment that could come only after thorough discussion. It challenges every person involved to search his or her own heart and to search Holy Scripture. The best question shuts the mouth of opponents graciously because it leads to changed thinking and believing. It also leads to meaningful solutions because it goes to the heart of the matter.

If we keep at the forefront of our minds the goals of loving God and loving neighbor, our churches will more and more reflect the glory and power of the gospel of Jesus Christ (Mark 8:35; Luke 6:27–28). If we never forget that our witness to the world will be only as strong as our relationships and unity within the church (John 17:20–23), then we will work hard as laypeople and leaders to develop and protect authentic relationships (Rom. 14:19; Heb. 12:14). Remembering the extent of our forgiveness in Christ should compel us to forgive others (Eph. 4:32). Then we will labor intently at peacemaking to maintain the unity of the Spirit through the bond of peace (Eph. 4:1–3).

Keeping these biblical goals in mind while walking through church conflicts will help us not only respond biblically to the immediate circumstances we are facing, but establish a pattern for life that is God-centered and eternity-focused. *Redeeming church conflicts requires the reframing of the conflict into eternal (best) questions.* Making these best questions the central topics for discussion is one important aspect of the redemption process. Best questions will help resolve both personal and material conflicts.

What Best Questions Do

Over the years, we have listened to, counseled, and prayed with hundreds of concerned and hurting Christians. The exact details of each conversation are always unique, but our counsel is the same: "Take heart, Christian! Remember eternity and have hope. Get your eyes off yourself and your circumstance and fix them firmly on the Triune God." Of course, God's Word communicates these truths far better than our words. Therefore we often have them read from the book of Job and ask them to reflect specifically on the questions that God asked Job.

> Then the LORD answered Job out of the storm. He said: "Who is this that darkens my counsel with words without knowledge? Brace yourself like a man; I will question you, and you shall answer me.
> "Where were you when I laid the earth's foundation? Tell me, if you understand. Who marked off its dimensions? Surely you know! Who stretched a measuring line across it? On what were its footings set, or who laid its cornerstone—while the morning stars sang together and all the angels shouted for joy?" (Job 38:1–7)

In one particularly challenging church conflict call, I (Dave) remember asking a seasoned church leader, Pastor Thomas, to read and then explain this passage to me. Pastor Thomas was so agitated and despairing at the beginning of our call that initially I wondered if we would be able to make any progress at all. But this man was a true believer. The Spirit of God rested in him and was clearly at work. As we prayed together, discussed his conflicted church, and studied Scripture together, we reflected on how God had consented to Job's demand for a face-to-face meeting so that Job could "give free rein to [his] complaint" (10:1). Then God pointed out something we all need to remember when faced with a difficult situation. God reminded Job that his perspective is bigger and fuller than ours. His response in chapter 38 did not address the specifics of Job's complaint. Rather, he confronted Job with eternity. Job comes to God with his "why" questions and in response, God asks, "Where were you when I laid the earth's foundation?" God was demanding a change in Job's viewpoint; he was demanding the same change from this hurting pastor. God calls for a viewpoint shift in all of us as we seek to redeem our church conflicts.

Churches remain conflicted because they have lost their perspective and failed to ask the best questions of the parties involved. Putting church conflicts, no matter how painful they might be, in the context of eternity—just as God put Job's complaint in perspective—will begin to change radically how we view conflict. Temporal concerns in conflicts will always triumph over the unseen concerns of faith unless the church becomes intentionally more effective at fostering deep, lasting, *heart and attitude changes*, often cultivated through best questions that prioritize the value of eternal grace above that of the wealth and benefits of the world.

By the end of our call, Pastor Thomas realized that he had been operating on the temporal plane and started focusing on the eternal, where his true hope resided. His church conflicts remained problematic, frustrating, and painful, but God is still the same as he was yesterday, even in the middle of the conflict. He had saved, redeemed, forgiven, and adopted Pastor Thomas into the family of God; and God was at work in his heart, sanctifying him and growing him in conformity to Christ. No, all of the substantive conflicts in his church were not yet resolved, but Pastor Thomas was encouraged by remembering that God's Word was sufficient to help him with this conflict and help his other leaders and all the laypeople as well. Remembering these truths about God, the church, and all of the means of grace available through Christ reorients our perspective, reframes the presenting issues into best questions, and enables us to walk *redemptively* through conflict. The best questions point us to an eternal perspective and move us from despair to hope.

Sample Best Questions

Sometimes we will ask best questions that will reveal new information or suggest creative solutions. At other times, a best question will simply (and appropriately) slow down the process and reorient the participants involved to a God-centered focus. As one example of this, I (Tara) asked an apparent best question of a pastor who was emotionally and antagonistically overreacting to a conflict in his church. After listening to him for nearly twenty minutes as he spouted off passionate, pointed accusations, I simply asked, "Pastor, would you please pray for our conversation?"

This simple question stopped him in his tracks. Just the discipline of praying for a few moments helped remind him of who God is, who he is (a child of God, a shepherd-pastor), and who the other people involved are (fellow brothers and sisters in Christ, his sheep). Other examples of questions that may be best questions in your church's conflict include the following:

- What don't we know and what aren't we doing in the church to avoid misunderstandings? Do we trust each other consistently as eternal "image bearers" and "joint heirs" so that we are being intentional about communicating with respect and care for others?
- Do we want, as a first priority, what Jesus wants? Do our values, goals, gifts, calling, priorities, expectations, interests, or opinions align with those of the Lord Jesus? Because we can see in Scripture that the church cannot function and be complete without the exercise of different spiritual gifts by different people (1 Cor. 12:12–31), are we gracious advocates for the development and use of those gifts in the church?
- As stewards are we using the resources we have available for ministry in a manner consistent with God's priorities for the building of his church? What more do we need to know about God's priorities so we can use our resources in a manner consistent with his revealed will for the church?
- When fellow Christians' attitudes and desires lead to sinful words and actions, how can we help change them? We are called to be faithful servants by holding accountable for their sins those fellow children of God who bring conflict to our church due to their own passions and desires. How do we do this? What does it mean to be a holy person in a holy church?

In 1979 when I attended a Francis Schaeffer conference, I (Dave) saw a brilliant example of asking best questions. A woman in the audience asked a complicated question, which Schaeffer patiently repeated. But then he did something remarkable. He didn't answer her question; rather, he taught her how to ask the best question. First, he explained that actually her question contained three questions and that each of the three questions contained presuppositions that were aimed at directing his response. Thus, if he responded only to her initial inquiry, he would not be answering her true—*best*—question. Then he restated the woman's three questions stripped of presuppositions and asked her if those were the questions she would like him to answer. When she said yes, he gave his honest answers to those redefined questions.

Now I do not remember the actual questions or answers Schaeffer gave but I remember well the lesson of the mental process we should follow when forming a question and when responding to a question. Not all questions are worthy of answers. Asking best questions leads to best responses.

A Mini Case Study

A pastor we conflict-coached had the responsibility for the biblical education of his leaders and members for a period of ten years. He was suddenly and unexpectedly (he reported) asked to resign—an indication to us that he had failed in his teaching task. Rather than focusing on his feelings of being "crushed and scared" and "angry and resentful," the first question we encouraged the pastor to ask himself was, *Where did I fail in my teaching of these leaders and members?* If the pastor was faithfully teaching the whole of Scripture, he would have taught that a pastor is a called shepherd of God's people and not merely a "hired hand" to be disposed of like a common laborer in a secular job (John 10:12–13).

The pastor had obviously failed to teach what it means to be called to ministry. A call is not merely something perceived by the pastor as the one called, but it is equally as binding an action on those who issued the call and therefore cannot easily be laid aside by either party as is done in the secular world. Of course many pastors would not have the spiritual maturity in the emotion of their self-centered hurt to think in these terms. So the real question for us was, How do we help this pastor grow spiritually through this experience? Similarly, how do we help these leaders and members come to understand the biblical message of what it means to be called to the ministry?

One of the first steps in redeeming church conflict is data gathering. Some of the best questions and considerations in this particular conflict were these:

- Was there really no indication whatsoever of a reason for the termination? It seemed unlikely that such would be the case. Pastors are terminated because of personality type, actual pastoral misconduct, and many things in between. The pastor needed to be confronted gently to explore any possible cause that could lie behind such an action. One of the best questions that could be asked in this conflict was: Did the pastor fail to educate the church on the biblical meaning of pastoral call and the appropriate process for removing a pastor from office?

- What was the actual authority of those who have taken the action of termination as described here? This question concerns the church's polity structure. What did the bylaws say concerning both process and implementation of such a decision? Is this church under the oversight of another ecclesiastical body (presbytery, conference, district) that can be appealed to for both procedural and substantive due process considerations? Answers to these questions will determine what additional questions need to be asked of both the pastor and the leaders and members who have taken this action.

- What did the church leaders and members understand the phrase "called to the ministry" to mean? Did it mean just a call to this one local church or is it something far broader than that? Again this is a data-gathering question for both pastor and leaders and members. If it becomes clear that a mere "hired hand" mentality is pervasive (see again John 10:12–13 and our further discussion of hired hand in chap. 10), both pastor and leaders/members should be confronted with the nature of such an unbiblical and ungodly attitude.

- Why, Pastor, were you feeling crushed, scared, angry, resentful, and devastated? His answers will provide valuable insight into what he believes it means to trust God and what God may be doing in his spiritual life that has apparently become dependent on the actions and decisions of mere men. What was God doing? Do you believe he is sovereign over all things? Not only what might he be teaching you but what does he want this congregation to learn as they pursue this action? Data-gathering questions like these help ascertain the person's depth of calling and their biblical understanding of ministry.

- Asking him, "How have you contributed to this situation?" will also be an eye-opener. If he says "nothing," there is likely some serious denial going on. If he begins to provide serious

94

and meaningful answers, this data will later be used to help him form appropriate confessions, which can be used to demonstrate to the leaders and members his contributions to the conflict.

These best questions helped us develop an appropriate conflict-coaching and mediation plan for the pastor, his wife, and the leaders and members of the church. The plan followed the pattern of the Four Gs of Peacemaking in Ken Sande's book *The Peacemaker,* which we introduced in chapter 2 and will discuss further in section 4.

Above all of these questions is the preeminent call for all of the people involved in the church conflict (pastor, leaders, and members) to remember that this is God's church, not theirs to be done with as they please. Jesus was about reconciling us to the Father; therefore, we should be about reconciling ourselves with each other. If that message can be absorbed, there is hope that God's agenda of growth in holiness in every person involved will be realized.

Apply This to Your Church Conflict

Of all the skills you will develop as you co-labor with Christ to redeem your church's conflicts, learning to ask best questions will be near the top of the list of the most difficult things you will do. The conflict may be defined and perceived in many different ways by the parties involved. Applying the instruction of the Bible to each party (individual or sub-group) may mean unraveling multiple conflicts through multiple assessments. The tangled web of group conflict in many church disagreements presents one of the most challenging peacemaking environments imaginable. Consider just a few factors that make group conflicts complex:

- Sinful man's inability to perceive rightly (blindness).
- The propensity we all have to rationalize surface (presenting) issues.
- The church's culture as it is influenced by its polity.
- The need to take seriously the anxiety of church leaders and members.

The authority of God's Word will address these complexities and be persuasive; human wisdom alone will not suffice. Asking best questions in thorough discussion with others in the church helps us live in accordance with God's call to be people with renewed minds (see Rom. 12:2). By relying on Scripture—the real source of true wisdom—you can develop the confidence required to see through the complexity of church conflict by asking best questions. This will help you develop *knowledge* and *perseverance* as you gain hope for the redemption of conflict. "Add to your faith goodness; and to goodness, knowledge; and to knowledge, self-control; and to self-control, perseverance" (2 Peter 1:5–6).

Questions for Reflection

1. As you consider everything going on in your church, what is the best question (or series of questions) you can ask yourself right now that will change how you respond to these conflicts?
2. Trusting God in conflict can become a unifying movement that draws people away from narrow self-centeredness. What have you done or are you planning to do that will show others that you trust God with the situation?
3. How would the conflicts at your church change if everyone, including you, remembered consistently that the church is God's and not the property or domain of any human person or group?

Recommended Resources for Further Study

Jerry Bridges, *Trusting God: Even When Life Hurts* (Colorado Springs: NavPress, 1988).

Edmund P. Clowney, *Called to the Ministry* (Phillipsburg, NJ: P&R Publishing, 1976).

Charles Dunahoo, *Making Kingdom Disciples* (Phillipsburg, NJ: P&R Publishing, 2006).

Paul David Tripp, *Instruments in the Redeemer's Hands: People in Need of Change Helping People in Need of Change* (Phillipsburg, NJ: P&R Publishing, 2002).

7

....

Working with Church Groups

Stop listening to instruction, my son, and you will stray from the words of knowledge.

Proverbs 19:27

I know that you believe you understand what you think I said, but I'm not sure you realize that what you heard is not what I meant.

Robert McCloskey, U.S. State Department spokesperson
during the Vietnam War

If you have ever been in a congregational meeting right before a church splits, you know that gentle, wise, productive discussion filled with careful listening is not usually the norm. When a group is severely conflicted, careful communication is usually at an all-time low. Lifetime friends are shocked to find themselves as opponents because they are consumed by the pull and force of competing groups. Someone dusts off corporate documents for the first time in decades for the purpose of discovering a weapon with which to defeat opponents, not seeking unity but victory.

It doesn't have to be this way. Instead, just as in the early church in Acts 15, church conflicts can be redeemed by careful listening, an important aspect of group interaction. "The whole assembly became silent as they listened to Barnabas and Paul telling about the miraculous signs and wonders God had done among the Gentiles through them" (Acts 15:12).

To listen carefully during a church conflict, it is helpful to understand some basic principles of group agendas, group dynamics, and church polity. What follows will help you understand what is going on, as you participate in meetings and discussions, and will help you see more clearly how you, as a co-laborer with Christ, can help redeem conflict.

Group Agendas

The term *conflict* as used in this book is derived from James 4, which links the concept of loss of peace with an individual's desires. That desire may be a conscious desire-driven decision or it may be something as abstract as a mere feeling or intuition. When that desire goes unsatisfied in an individual, however, the result can be anything from mild frustration to deep-seated anger. At the heart of not having one's desires satisfied is often a sense of loss—loss of control, loss of personal identity, loss of ability to craft one's own course, and so on.

In a group conflict, people with perceived similar agendas may band together out of a sense of empowerment, or at least a sense of potential empowerment. A group sharing a goal (desire) will define their common interests in such a way that they will hopefully prevail over other competing groups. Frequently positions and interests held by groups in conflict are also driven by individual fears related to what others in the group may think of them. This "fear of man" agenda adds another level of complexity to the group conflict equation: as individuals desire to be accepted within their own group, they will further isolate themselves from other groups.

Fear of man can also be mixed with genuine love and loyalty to those who have cared for us, sat by us in church, and visited us when others have not. Thus there can be a strong sense of obligation not to betray or desert these loyal friends, even when we may become convinced that our understanding of the conflict was wrong. The desire to be accepted by and loyal to a group of people can become even more powerful than the original desire that started the conflict.

Another group agenda has to do with competing groups seeking to define and align their desires with what they believe is "God's agenda." Therefore a group will justify extreme measures to accomplish their goals, and a sense of a "holy crusade" can easily develop. When two groups in the same church declare that their differing positions are God's agenda, it is obvious that they both cannot accurately be representing God's position, interests, and plan for the church. At least one is wrong (or at least not totally right), or both of them are wrong. When Christians fight over their desires, almost always they misrepresent God's agenda and, therefore, fall into sin. This is the trap of spiritual adultery spoken of in James 4:4–5 that is actually driven by world-centered desires rather than God-centered desires.

Group conflicts between Christians are resolved when everyone's desires and agendas align with God's desires and agendas. Pride is usually a more powerful force in human conflict than the delayed future satisfaction of eternal values, and it blinds us from clearly seeing God's agenda. This pride may be extremely hard to detect—it may look like fighting for something important and right. It may look like devotion to God but is actually fear of man. And in every situation where sinful pride is present, there are always other motivations and agendas too—some godly, some not.

Group Dynamics

In a normal mediation, there are just two parties, or sometimes a very small group of people like a family, two sets of couples, or one boss and a handful of subordinates. Most church conflicts require other types of dispute resolution in addition to mediation. For example, when we serve a conflicted church, we always begin with an in-depth intake process before we arrive on-site. Then we spend days serving in complicated conflict-coaching appointments when we work one-on-one with individuals. These coaching appointments lead inevitably to small mediations (between two or three people) and larger group mediations (working among tens if not hundreds of people simultaneously). It takes prayer, skill, and extensive time to work through conflict-coaching and both small and large mediations, but the group mediations are particularly difficult due to a number of factors in group dynamics: the problems of a stage and a mob mentality, the refusal to take personal responsibility, the fear of man, and the root of all of these, failure of group leadership.

Stage and Mob Mentality

Most people, willingly or not, act differently when put before an audience. In group mediation the person speaking for his or her side is on a stage. This person has been given a platform from which to demonstrate to the others that he or she is zealous for the cause of that side. Frequently people in this position use hyperbole to make a point, which causes the opposition to hear only the extremes and not whatever truth may have been presented.

A "mob mentality" feeds into the problems associated with people speaking from a stage. When mob mentality takes over, people feel confirmed in their views, and cherished positions develop to the point of becoming almost unassailable demands. The rush of performing for others combined with the power of group-think can push people to feel justified and reasonable in their convictions, even if they may have self-doubts or secret concerns.

Self-doubt of the conscience can be a valuable check on excess, but this restraint is often overcome when other people take an even more unreasonable position. The temptations associated with a mob mentality and being on stage in church conflicts can lead people to do and say things in groups that, on their own, in private, they never would do and say. Personal attacks, caustic words, championing the loudest, most convincing person (rather than the humble, gentle, servant leader) begin to reign, as Christian principles and Christian character are ignored and devalued.

Lack of Personal Responsibility

At some point in most church conflicts, we will hear people say something along the lines of, "This conflict is not about me. I'm just a representative of a group of a whole bunch of people who think like me." Even well-meaning Christians with deep theological training will try to keep any mediation efforts focused away from their hearts. They will claim that the conflict is *only* about material issues, not about their sinful desires, words, and actions. The truth, however, is usually that *both* material and personal issues are present whenever groups are conflicted. Even if people start out only as representatives of the positions of the conflicted groups, they rarely remain there. People may try to justify their harshness because of the "ministry seriousness" involved, but Scripture calls us to be kind and not quarrelsome in our communications (see 2 Tim. 2:24–26) and to avoid unwholesome talk (see Eph. 4:29).

Fear of Man

When individuals in groups are motivated by fear of the opinion of other people (what others personally think about them) more than the fear of God, their hearts grow cold to the Spirit of God. Lacking God-consciousness, there is no restraining the motivation of the heart; only worldly passions and popularity with the crowd control. This is common in church conflicts. Defensiveness, self-righteousness, and pride rule the day when people give in to the fear of man.

Failure of Group Leadership

In each of the group dynamic situations listed above, one of the primary things being revealed is a failure of leadership. God calls spiritual leaders to lead his people into the place where all interests of man are subservient to God's interests (see Phil. 2:1–4). Leaders are called to help people understand the dangerous dynamics discussed above so they can be avoided in the future and repented of if already present. If they have the trust of those they lead, the place of responsibility for decisions will properly be set in their hands. But if leaders have failed to lead, attempts at congregational meetings or group discussions usually break down or one side capitulates to the other on important material issues. The need for the gospel of Jesus Christ as the only remedy for sin is forgotten or devalued. Frequently there is no personal reconciliation and God's interests are ignored.

Group conflicts are best resolved when people follow humble, godly leaders and the decisions these leaders reach during private mediation processes. Leaders participating in private mediations have the opportunity to change personally because the dynamics of the stage and mob are not present, and fear of man can be confronted as a counseling issue. Then leaders who change are able to call the people of the congregation to follow their lead and forsake private interests for the sake of the church and the glory of God. It takes courage, humility, and gentleness to be a spiritual leader in the Lord's church, particularly when it is in conflict.

A Mini Case Study

An example of the impact of group agendas and group dynamics in church conflict was experienced when I (Dave) led a team of mediators tasked with reconciling a number of churches and a Christian school. The material issues were many and complex, but the personal issues were particularly hurtful to all involved—especially the children and parents who loved both their school and their churches. Twelve churches were involved in the conflict, in addition to the church that had originally founded the school years earlier.

To help the groups involved, we had to first help identify with them the issues and the underlying interests. The broad topics included governance and personal, legal, and structural issues. The positions on the issues were legion. As I went back and forth between the two groups during their time of private caucus, I quickly saw the dilemma and reasons for confusion. Each group had serious *internal* disagreements about their positions and the reasons behind them. Within one camp, there was no agreement on what was important or unimportant or the reasons behind their positions. The longer they stayed in their respective groups and thoroughly discussed the topics, the more clearly they saw their own internal differences. Off the stage, without the mob mentality pressuring them to posture and strut, everyone involved began to discern that even their supposedly unified groups were not that unified. (In fact, two men inside one of the groups were so conflicted, we had to schedule an extensive mediation to work through their conflicts—and they were supposedly on the same side!)

Ultimately it took five full days of discussion to capture all of the issues, positions, and interests, but the effort was worth it. By the end of our time on-site, both church and school leaders saw for the first time how unified (or close to unified) they actually were on nine-tenths of the material issues. They signed an agreement covering governance issues in the realm of the school and what issues were under the authority of the founding church. And together, they agreed on a road map for working through unresolved open issues—including the need for repentance, confession, and forgiveness by many of the people involved.

Church Polity—Governance

One aspect of group dynamics that should be considered as you work through your church's conflicts is the *governance structure* of your particular church, also known as *polity*. Even if you have never formally studied church polity or read the organizing documents of your local congregation, you will need to be sensitive to your church's authority structure as you consider in a conflict what steps to take, with whom to speak, and what resources you may have beyond your local church leaders.

What we offer here is far from a thorough discussion of this complex topic, but our aim is to provide the terminology and a general overview that should be sufficient for you to discern your church's governance and authority structure and to think through the issues that are applicable to your church's conflict.

There are three fundamental forms of polity: prelacy (also known as episcopal), presbyterian, and congregational. In prelacy, the local church is administered by a distinct category of church officers often known as priests, with bishops over them; final decision-making authority is frequently found outside the local church.

Presbyterian polity recognizes the right of the local congregation to elect elders to an elder body (the local governing body of elders, which may be called a session, consistory, or council). The pastor or minister is one of the elders with equal stature and authority with lay elders. Corporately the elder body has governing authority over the local church; however, elders are also members of a regional presbytery or classis, which has authority over several churches in a region. Furthermore, some of the members of a presbytery are members of a general assembly (or synod), which has authority over all of the churches in a nation or large region.

Congregationally run churches practice multiple forms of congregational polity. Some have a single elder (the pastor) and a board of elected deacons who serve under his authority (the form most commonly found in Baptist churches), while others have an elected elder board on which the pastor serves as one of many (a form found in many independent Bible churches). In a true congregational independency, every church is independent from every other, with internal decision-making authority usually divided between the officers and the members. In an extreme form of congregationalism the members may vote on every decision.

A complicating factor related to polity is that, while a system of church governance may have been formally adopted and stand as part of the bylaws, actual practice may not follow it. Over time the church may have deviated substantially from its own governing documents.

Thus, as you consider how the Lord is calling you to redeem your church's conflicts, consider how your church's polity affects your course of action. As you do so, remember that you may have to consider both how your church should respond according to the polity as stated in its organizing documents and how your church actually functions in real life.

A Mini Case Study

One example of how polity played into the group dynamics of a church that I (Dave) assisted was when the core issue concerned making the transition from a congregational form of governance to a presbyterian polity. For most of the old-timers, the thought of losing congregationalism was equivalent to losing their church. They truly believed that if elders were in charge, then elitists would take over and selfishly let power go to their heads, all to the detriment (if not destruction) of their church. Their concerns were not completely unwarranted, as anyone who has ever seen a leader abuse his or her authority could tell you.

So before any material issues could even be considered, the people had to come to terms with their fundamental heart issue: fear. They were so afraid of what *might* happen to "their" church that they were forgetting whose church it was (God's). Of course helping them look into their hearts was particularly challenging because they were not used to following or trusting the guidance of any leaders—so the acceptance of our efforts as mediators was even slower than usual. It took additional time to educate the entire congregation and work with leaders to help them all work through the change process.

Eventually members began to see the biblical basis for elders they would choose so that appropriate decision-making authority and shepherding responsibilities could be clearly established. Much of the decision had to be based on what people could trust about God and his call on able leaders who would act on his behalf as servants in the church. That came only as they moved from self-interest and a desire for control to faith that God would govern their church through those committed to his interests. The process was one of growing in spiritual maturity as the concept of trust took on an entirely new meaning for these people.

Apply This to Your Church Conflict

As you consider how group dynamics and group agendas are contributing to conflict, it may seem easy to identify the various competing groups. (Generally, screaming people who are about to resort to physical punches give themselves away.) But it may take extensive effort to understand the nuances related to your church's group dynamics and agendas. Consider carefully how many people in your church you have something against and have not forgiven. Further consider how many people in your church you believe have something against you and have not forgiven you. This will help you identify the factions and groups associated with your church's conflicts.

Always remember that personal reconciliation is the only way to have group reconciliation because group conflicts are rooted in individual conflicts. A *group* can't be reconciled, but individuals *can*. What this really boils down to is one person, created in God's image, living a redeemed life in a fallen world. This person must, in one way or another, deal with his or her relationship with God and others based on that new status. And then, as these individual persons deal with their relationships with others, there can be peace, reconciliation, and unity. Big changes can grow out of small acts of faithfulness!

Questions for Reflection

1. Are you a good listener? Do you interrupt people or do you concentrate on what the speaker is saying? If you consider yourself an attentive listener, what evidence would you present as proof of your good listening skills?
2. If you don't get what you want in the resolution of your church's present conflicts, what will you do? Why?
3. When you consider the phrase "fear of man," what comes to mind? Do your thoughts include just physical fear of another person or, more appropriately, the fear you may have of not being favorably accepted by someone or some group? What do you intend to do about it?

Recommended Resources for Further Study

Steven B. Cowan, ed., *Who Runs the Church? Four Views on Church Government* (Grand Rapids: Zondervan, 2004).

Wayne A. Mack and David Swavely, *Life in the Father's House* (Phillipsburg, NJ: P&R Publishing, 1996).

Colin Marshall and Tony Payne, *The Trellis and the Vine: The Ministry Mind-Shift That Changes Everything* (Youngstown, OH: Matthias Media, 2009).

John Stott, *Basic Christian Leadership: Biblical Models of Church, Gospel and Ministry* (Downers Grove, IL: InterVarsity, 2006).

8

··

Moving from Spiritual
Blindness to Sight

So justice is far from us, and righteousness does not reach us. We look for light, but all is darkness; for brightness, but we walk in deep shadows. Like the blind we grope along the wall, feeling our way like men without eyes.

Isaiah 59:9–10

One of the tragic effects of the Fall is personal blindness. . . . It is universal.

Paul Tripp

Even though everything Peter, Paul, and Barnabas stated in Acts 15 lined up with the Old Testament Scriptures that had been around for a thousand years, some were blind to the message of the gospel and where it was intended to go.

The words of the prophets are in agreement with this, as it is written: "After this I will return and rebuild David's fallen tent. Its ruins I will rebuild, and I will restore it, that the remnant of men may seek the Lord, and all the Gentiles who bear my name, says the Lord, who does these things" that have been known for ages. (Acts 15:15–18)

Some were blind to the truths that had been foretold to the prophets centuries ago. This kind of blindness is not physical; it is spiritual. Scripture uses the terms *blind* and *blindness* as a spiritual metaphor to describe a condition that renders a person unable to discern spiritual truth. Spiritually blind persons can think they are just fine but they are actually incapable of comprehending the true meaning of spiritual things. They may be able to "see" some truth but be completely blind to other aspects of God's revelation.

Don't be surprised by the spiritual blindness that exists in church conflict. Most of us need help to see the truths in the Bible and the people involved in your church conflict will need help to see their blindness. The physically blind have a distinct advantage over the spiritually blind—they know they are blind. Usually the spiritually blind person cannot make an accurate self-diagnosis of his or her condition. And we all, to one degree or another, are spiritually blind. The greatest challenge we face as we seek to redeem our conflicts is in overcoming personal spiritual blindness. It colors every aspect of how we see every situation. Not only that, every other person in our church, leader and member alike, suffers from the same disability.

Personal spiritual blindness leads us into conflict and binds us to conflict. It is a major contributor to keeping our deepest desires hidden beneath the seemingly important issues in our conflict. It also leads to our condemning others as we attack them with accusations concerning their blind spots, while not once considering our own. In church conflicts one of the key indicators of corporate blindness is the frequent hurling of accusations about the blindness of others ("They don't understand the real issues"; "He is out of touch with what he did and the effect it is having on others"; and so on). Redeeming church conflicts can happen only when we stop accusing and start asking God to search us, to reveal our own blindness.

We ought to *assume* our own blindness and pray that God would use the conflict to reveal our skewed desires and motivations, which lie hidden beneath our actions and words. We can do this by praying earnestly the prayer of Psalm 139:23–24: "Search me, O God, and know my heart; test me and know my anxious thoughts. See if there is any offensive way in me, and lead me in the way everlasting."

The Masks of Spiritual Blindness

Paul Tripp addresses the condition of spiritual blindness as well as anyone we know. He writes:

> A spiritually blind person not only fails to recognize his blindness, he is convinced that he has excellent vision. A fundamental part of being spiritually blind is that you are blind to your blindness. Spiritual blindness is deceptive. Spiritual blindness is deceptive because it masquerades as other things. If we are going to be God's instruments to open blind eyes [including our own], we must recognize the typical masks that spiritual blindness wears.[1]

The masks of personal blindness that Tripp describes are numerous, masks "of an accurate assessment of self, of being sinned against, of trials and testing, of needs, of wise counsel, of personal insight, of a sense of values, of theological knowledge, of personal holiness, and of repentance."[2] As shocking as the discovery may be that we wear any one of these masks, our awareness of them should force us into serious self-examination and then repentance. Once submitted and admitted to God, our blinders will begin to fall off and we will be better equipped to gently help others deal with their blindness and spiritual shortcomings.

In church conflicts, one of the most predominant and serious forms of both individual and corporate blindness is that of a "sense of values." I (Dave) worked on a case several years ago where the mask of a sense of values was displayed.

Jim thought he knew what was important, but the more I listened to him the more convinced I became that what moved him were not the things of prime importance. Jim was displaying a form of blindness. He had evaluated his situation in the church's conflict and acted in a way consistent with his values, yet his and the church's problems continued. This left him frustrated, confused, and at times angry.

All the treasures that motivated Jim had to do with what he considered the proper form of worship practiced at the church, and thus the form of worship became his idol, while in reality for Jim the substance of worship became unimportant. This personally valued form was at the core of his relationship, not only with God but also with other people in the church. And his demands based on this sense of values were contributing to a culture of conflict at the church. And Jim was one of the pastors!

He entered relationships with a long list of silent demands centered on his core value, yet he was unaware of how judgmental and unforgiving he was when people failed to live up to it. Jim saw relationships through the narrow lens of his values, and he evaluated all others on the basis of their agreement or disagreement with them. Basically he ignored those with different values in this area.

Fortunately for Jim, many in the church agreed with his value of a certain form of worship. In fact, in this church, many, like their pastor, valued the form the worship service took more highly than the substance of God's truth that was presented.

Churches of all sizes, traditions, geographic locales, and socio-economic statuses can value form over substance in worship style. Some churches try to be "seeker-sensitive" or "seeker-driven" by adopting popular music and predominately serving up friendly, ear-pleasing messages. Other churches pride themselves in practicing only archaic forms of Puritan-like worship with solemn hymns and long serious sermons. Either can be driven by their chosen form rather than by God's substantive values to include the changing of man's heart for the sake of Christ.

Matthew 6 says that whatever is my treasure will control my heart, and what controls my heart will control my behavior. In other words, I will live to gain, maintain, and enjoy the things that are of value to me. Jim's problem was his view of his values and his worship of them. Frequently Jim was in conflict with others because their values didn't align with his, but he didn't recognize his blindness because it was masked by a passionate sense of what was right worship and what was wrong worship. It is easy to be deceived into thinking that you are rightly worshiping God when you worship worship.

Jim failed to see that God was using many of his relationships to chip away at the dross in Jim's character, and this became frustrating for him. God's focus was not on the form of worship that Jim so dearly loved but on Jim's sanctification, but Jim was blind to the process God was using to conform him to Christ. His blindness fueled the conflicts in his church. Yes, there were other sources of conflict, but this was one major contributor. It was a personal heart problem for Jim that became a whole church problem. The corporate blindness that trapped this church was a form of blindness we call form over substance.

In another example of blindness, I (Tara) conflict-coached with a woman who started our conversation with so much fury and vehemence, *my* heart rate rose in response. As she flung accusation after accusation with uncharitable presumptions galore, I could only marvel at the depth of her anger. But soon I realized that she was completely blind to her heart's anger. She kept making statements like "I'm not angry" and "I *used to be angry.*" She might as well have been saying, "I can fly to the moon." Her blindness took her far from reality, and my task was to help her understand her heart's misplaced motivation.

I did what I always do in such conversations. I prayed that the eyes of her heart would be opened. And I asked her gentle questions to encourage her to see God, the situation, the other person, and her own heart accurately. Thankfully, even though she started our conversation with her eyes totally closed, soon her eyes were opened just a little bit—and then a little bit more. And by the end of our interaction, not only did she see how angry she was, she knew the next steps she should take to turn away from her sin.

The Hypocrisy of Blindness

Matthew 15:1–20 addresses how our blindness can lead us into hypocrisy. In our spiritual blindness, we often say and do things that conflict with what we say we believe as Christians—and that is hypocrisy. In this passage Jesus carefully contrasts the low value he places on outward rules and forms with his value for heart change that rejects anything by which man will "nullify the word of God for the sake of your tradition" (v. 6). Please take a moment to read all of Matthew 15:1–20; then consider your own personal blindness about traditions that may be contributing to your church's present conflicts. Say to yourself: *I know God is at work in my life to redeem this situation for his glory and my growth, so what is he doing and why am I not recognizing it?* We agree with Paul Tripp that "this question can lead to greater insight, biblical change, and a harvest of good fruit."[3]

Please remember that we can mask our spiritual blindness in many ways. Real discernment comes as masks are revealed and removed through the sanctifying work of God that frees us from the disability of spiritual blindness. Discernment develops not only as we discover and know our opponent's issues, positions, and underlying interests but also as we uncover the various masks of blindness we wear to distort the truth. Hebrews 5:14 says, "But solid food is for the mature, who by constant use have trained themselves to distinguish good from evil." Your power of discernment develops as you constantly eat the "solid food" of Scripture. Dealing with personal spiritual blindness requires a heart bent on turning to Jesus (the Light) so that we may know the whole truth about ourselves and others; only then are we ready to redeem our church's conflicts.

Sanctification Opens Our Eyes

Sanctification is the ongoing process of growth in holiness as Christians become increasingly Christlike. Through sanctification, the fruit of the Spirit becomes the very character of the Christian. Sanctification is an ongoing cooperative process in which the true believer, free from sin's domination, makes an effort to live in a manner obedient to God's Word and obedient to Christ's commands. But it is a "God-dependent effort" (J. I. Packer's expression), so the Christian knows that his own efforts alone would amount to nothing. We know the work of redeeming church conflict is of God; however, it is also of us, as we cooperate with what he is doing in such conflicts to effect change in us. Church conflict is an amazingly rich opportunity for God-dependent effort.

In our church's conflict, we are called to resist the flesh and fulfill the call of the enabling Spirit by refusing to sin in the face of the temptation to remain blind and to win. That God-dependent effort is the effort that will open our eyes. Rather than merely prevailing in an argument, we will seek to redeem conflict for both the glory of God and the sanctification of those believers who participate in that effort. If even one person in the church accepts this call to the work of redeeming church conflicts, his or her eyes will be opened and growth in grace will occur. Also sanctification opens the doors for others to follow suit, turn away from blindness, and grow in their faith and holiness. Exposing blindness, personally and corporately, is a fruit of our redemption in Christ.

Church conflict is the seedbed, the growth environment, in which we can mature if we turn the opportunity of redeeming our church's conflicts into opportunities for "mining" spiritual growth. God has promised to conform us to the image of his Son (Rom. 8:28–29). Nothing can thwart God's promises or purposes. He will use everything, even the unique realm of church conflict, to grow his children in spiritual maturity and holiness. He has made us one in Christ. As believers in the gospel, we are all God's adopted children! And he is making us one in this life. We are all members of Christ's body and we are growing up into him who is our head (1 Cor. 12:27). As believers, because we are united in Christ, we are united to one another. One goal of this book is to provide a way for believers to live consistently with the reality of that unity—remembering that we belong to one another (Rom. 12:5).

God has something bigger and better for us than just surviving church conflict or making it go away. God is more concerned about what is going on in the heart of each person involved than about who will win or lose any particular debate or battle. And since God cares about our hearts—our maturing in Christ through sanctification, our turning away from being "ignoble" and becoming an "instrument for noble purposes . . . useful to the Master and prepared to do any good work" (2 Tim. 2:20–21)—we care about such things too. When we not only redeem our church conflicts but also live as peacemakers in the turmoil of church conflict, we are working with the Holy Spirit and living as sanctified instruments for noble purposes.

Apply This to Your Church Conflict

As you reflect on your church's present conflicts, consider the areas of blindness in your life and how God is calling you to *see more clearly*. Pray and ask God to give you a desire for spiritual sight. In the words of John Newton:

> There are many who stumble in the noon day, not for want of light, but for the want of eyes; and they who now see were once blind, even

as others, and had neither power nor will to enlighten their own minds. It is a mercy, however, when people are so far sensible of their own blindness, as to be willing to wait for the manifestation of the Lord's power, in the ordinances of His appointment.

He came into the world, and sends forth His Gospel, that those who see not, may see; and when there is a desire in the heart for spiritual sight, it shall in due time be answered.[4]

As we turn away from spiritual blindness, we remember who we are and whose we are. We see our sin and unbelief more clearly and we see the glory of God clearer still. Rather than blaming others for our church's conflict and focusing on them, we will see the culpability of our own hearts and how much we all are in need of God's grace.

Turning away from blindness will turn us away from self-righteousness and pride. We will remember anew that our identity is in Christ and that our eternity is secure. Even in the fire and trials of life in this world, we will be kept safe because God is with us. He provides all that we need for life and godliness in Christ (2 Peter 1:3). We do not have to be afraid. We do not have to cling to and grasp at worldly things. We can turn away from anxiety. God is in control and he is with us.

I will lead the blind by ways they have not known, along unfamiliar paths I will guide them; I will turn the darkness into light before them and make the rough places smooth. These are the things I will do; I will not forsake them. But those who trust in idols, who say to images, "You are our gods," will be turned back in utter shame. Hear, you deaf; look, you blind, and see! (Isaiah 42:16–18)

Questions for Reflection

1. "The greatest challenge you will face as you seek to redeem your conflicts is overcoming spiritual blindness." Do you agree with this statement? Why? If not, why not?
2. Have you been judgmental of others for having blind spots as they have reacted to your church's conflicts? What should that criticism tell you most about yourself?

3. What mask of spiritual blindness are you most prone to don when you face church conflict? Go over the list and be brutal in your self-analysis. Who can help you with recognizing your blindness, since by definition you cannot see it?

Recommended Resources for Further Study

Elyse Fitzpatrick, *Idols of the Heart* (Phillipsburg, NJ: P&R Publishing, 2001).

Kris Lundgaard, *The Enemy Within: Straight Talk about the Power and Defeat of Sin* (Phillipsburg, NJ: P&R Publishing, 1998).

Cornelius Plantinga Jr., *Not the Way It's Supposed to Be: A Breviary of Sin* (Grand Rapids: Eerdmans, 1995).

Section 3

Leadership

ACTS 15:7–35

Keep watch over yourselves and all the flock of which the Holy Spirit has made you overseers. Be shepherds of the church of God, which he bought with his own blood. I know that after I leave, savage wolves will come in among you and will not spare the flock. Even from your own number men will arise and distort the truth in order to draw away disciples after them. So be on your guard!

Acts 20:28–31

Faithful shepherds protect their flocks not only from harmful outside influences but from the self-serving among the sheep. Many congregations have experienced the intimidation of bullies within their midst when leaders fail to take responsibility to shepherd the flock. It is often the strong-willed, outspoken, highly opinionated folk who fill the void. There will always be leaders—the issue is whether they are the leaders called and gifted by God to shepherd his flock or those who push themselves forward so that they can push others around.

Timothy Z. Witmer

With a renewed eternal perspective and for the first time discerning the relevant issues and interests, the members of LCC next had to consider their Christian duties within the church. Specifically, each member and leader had an affirmative duty to one another; leaders had specific responsibilities related to their roles as shepherds; and every member (including leaders) had duties related to following and accountability. It was only as each person at LCC turned away from worldly ideas of individualism and autonomy that they began to live out Galatians 6:10: "Therefore, as we have opportunity, let us do good to all people, especially to those who belong to the family of believers."

At LCC doing good meant that most members and leaders began to respond to their church conflicts by using such words as "seeing my own heart idols" and asking questions such as, "What will please and honor the Lord in this situation?" These people were moving on to the next step of the Acts 15 model for redeeming church conflict: *responding biblically*. But sadly, as is almost always the case, some of the members rebelled.

These rebellious members were desperately in need of the ministry of *accountability*—speaking the truth in love through prayerful and redemptive church discipline. Thankfully, the other members and leaders of LCC were faithful to do this hard but necessary work of seeking accountability of all the members. The immediate fruit was a mixture of good and bad. Some people submitted to the accountability process, repented, and joined in the redemptive work of redeeming conflicts. Others renounced their church membership vows and sought to influence others to do likewise. After repeated efforts to reach out to these people, the elders and congregation were required by Scripture and by their love for God and these wayward people to formally excommunicate them from the church. This was done with much prayer, many tears, and every hope and expectation that such a step would communicate the severity of the hardness of heart being demonstrated by this small group. Some repented and the church rejoiced! But others retained an attorney and sued the church over the conflict and the discipline process. Our church conflict intervention team, working with the church's attorney, regularly had to remind LCC that God was sovereign and that even the lawsuit would be used to bring him glory and demonstrate his care for his people and his church.

Leadership determines not only the way a church's present conflicts are handled but also, in many cases, their outcome. Acts 15:7 says that it was after "much discussion" (affirming data gathering and broad participation in the expression of ideas) that Peter got up and exercised leadership. Other leaders did the same:

> After much discussion, Peter got up and addressed them. . . . The whole assembly became silent as they listened to Barnabas and Paul telling about the miraculous signs and wonders God had done among the Gentiles through them. When they finished, James spoke up. . . . Then the apostles and elders, with the whole church, decided to choose some of their own men and send them to Antioch with Paul and Barnabas. . . . The men were sent off and went down to Antioch, where they gathered the church together and delivered the letter. The people read it and were glad for its encouraging message. Judas and Silas, who themselves were prophets, said much to encourage and strengthen the brothers. After spending some time there, they were sent off by the brothers with the blessing of peace to return to those who had sent them. But Paul and Barnabas remained in Antioch, where they and many others taught and preached the word of the Lord. (Acts 15:7, 12–13, 22, 30–35)

We see Peter particularly bringing application of the Word of God (exemplifying authoritative leadership rather than authoritarian leadership) to the material issue of the conflict in Acts 15:7–11. Similarly, James, the half-brother of Jesus (an elder in the early church in Jerusalem), does the same thing a few verses later when he quotes Amos 9:11–12 (Acts 15:13–18). After carefully considering and discussing the issue, the leaders write a letter giving the church in Antioch clear direction as to what to do and expecting the Gentile believers to follow their guidance, especially in light of the nature of the controversy. The point is that pastors and church leaders must be capable of and willing to exercise confident, godly leadership in times of conflict; followers must be capable of and willing to follow.

Church conflicts are not resolved without the exercise of godly leadership and biblical followership. It's not accidental that Scripture refers to Christians as sheep needing a shepherd. The pastor facing conflict in his church needs affirmation to walk in the various leadership roles God has called him to in the church. These include discerning the present situation, managing the organization of details, prayerfully and strategically planning next steps, communicating clearly and decisively, teaching, and disciplining.

Pastors need encouragement to trust God with confidence and to lead biblically through church conflict. It was that element, after all, which led to the first church council's final decision—a decision, if not made, that could have led to a doctrine of salvation by works rather than by grace! Pastors and other church leaders need people, godly people, prepared by God to be biblical followers, an awesome responsibility in the church and equal in importance to leadership.

All members of a church (including all leaders) are called to be followers of Christ. Biblical followers pursue faithfully the lordship of Jesus. Without both followers and leaders on the same page as conflicts unfold, the benefits of redeeming our conflicts for God's glory will be lost and the church again put to shame. Too often in its history, perhaps even in the history of your own church, the name of Christ and the reputation of the church have been disgraced because conflicts were not resolved in a way that would show the power of the gospel to a watching world.

Issues tied to leadership are usually at the center of church conflict. There are many reasons for this. As in all authority relationships, those in the stronger position (church leaders) may be tempted to either abdicate their authority or warp it into sinful domination and control. And those in the weaker position (church members) may be tempted to undermine their leaders by refusing to submit to their authority or by trying to usurp authority through manipulative tactics. In this behavior both leaders and followers fail to love, pray for, protect, and encourage one another. All of these temptations work together to lay the groundwork for conflict in the church.

Sometimes when a leader is efficient and effective (strong with administrative details) or gifted as a teacher and preacher (strong intellectually), interpersonal skills are lacking. But some of the most relational people in the world struggle with organization and theological acumen. Problems arise when we expect everyone to be good at everything, rather than bearing with one another in our weaknesses and covering over with grace areas in need of further sanctification. Even more problems arise when we give in to the common temptation regarding leading and following in the church: either we put leaders on pedestals and never question, confront, or call them into account or we blame them for every problem in the church and forget that they, too, are fallible human beings like us.

Real church leaders have been given spiritual gifts of leadership, teaching, preaching, and discernment. Along with these gifts come duties. Leaders are in a strategic position to model ways to redeem their church's conflicts. Their personal example will have a huge impact on how their followers act. In addition, church leaders have unique ecclesiastical authority not only to encourage others to do the same but to discipline them if they don't. (Of course, this includes disciplining other leaders and being subject to discipline themselves.)

As we head into this discussion of leading and following in the church, we recognize that we are heading into a topic that is not only fraught with dangers but also so important and complicated that it cannot be fully addressed here. Still, we would be remiss if we did not do our best to at least point you in the direction of a number of foundational principles that you should consider regarding leaders, followers, and your church conflict.

9

Christian Duty within the Church

Do nothing out of selfish ambition or vain conceit, but in humility consider others better than yourselves. Each of you should look not only to your own interests, but also to the interests of others. Your attitude should be the same as that of Christ Jesus.

Philippians 2:3–5

Why can't you combine concern for repentance, etc. with concern for deep personal relationships? It seems to me that you have a duty. That duty is to make the ministry work. At the very least whether you work with them or not, you do have a duty to form a solid friendship with them and to learn from one another.

Jack Miller

Scripture calls us to authentic and committed relationships in the body of Christ. First John 1:7 calls us to have "fellowship with one another." In Galatians 2:9 the early Christians extended "the right hand of fellowship" to each other, and Philippians 1:5 calls us to "partnership in the gospel." In Acts 2:42 Christians "devoted themselves to the apostles' teaching and to the fellowship, to the breaking of bread and to prayer." In 1 Corinthians 12:26 we are reminded that when one in the body suffers, we all suffer.

Does this describe the relationships in your church? Many of us would say no, especially when our churches are conflicted. Rather than living out the call to love, most of us live to *be* loved. We are not committed to one another. Life is busy, conflicts come, and we move often. Online relationships and social networking may feel more real to us than our person-to-person relationships. We may live as though the grass really is greener in the next church but, when we find that grass is weed choked too, we flee for yet another church down the street. This level of relationship (or *lack* of relationship) completely forgets the Christian duty we have to one another in the church.

Just as Judas and Silas said much to encourage and strengthen the brothers (Acts 15:32), we have similar Christian duties to every person in our lives—leaders, followers, friends, foes, people under our authority and over us in authority. Our Christian duties are particularly important to remember when we face church conflicts. If we forget or ignore our duties, we will run away from conflict or attack one another. Our chief duty is to love each other (see Rom. 13:8 ; Gal. 5:6). The apostles and elders meeting at the first church council as reported in Acts 15 recognized their duty to the church by confronting conflict and providing encouragement and guidance.

Fulfilling Our Duty

What do I owe the person who differs from me? is the thinking pattern of duty. When all of the problems of a church conflict have been identified, and all of the various parties involved have been included, everyone must be called back to the fundamental question Jesus responds to in Matthew 22:36–40.

> "Teacher, which is the greatest commandment in the Law?" Jesus replied: "'Love the Lord your God with all your heart and with all your soul and with all your mind.' This is the first and greatest commandment. And the second is like it: 'Love your neighbor as yourself.' All the Law and the Prophets hang on these two commandments."

Our Lord teaches us to think in terms of duty, first our duty to God and then our duty to one another. In a church conflict, rarely is anyone thinking of duty from this perspective.

When we think of the concept of duty, various images come to mind:

- A soldier performing duties as a member of the armed forces
- A mother who must care for her child
- An employee who owes his employer a fair day's work

Frequently the motivation to do one's duty differs with the situation and the conscientiousness of the individual. In the above examples, the duty to be rendered could be based on the pure motive of true concern for those who would be adversely affected if the duty were not performed. But the motivation for performing the duty could also be based on fear—fear that should a duty not be performed, negative consequences might follow.

Consider the soldier. If he fails to do his duty, he could be court-martialed and imprisoned. He could be discharged from the service in disgrace. He could be financially penalized. The mother who fails in her duty toward her child could be charged with child abuse or reckless endangerment of a child, resulting in imprisonment. She could face divorce and the shame of being ostracized from her family and community. Or the employee who fails to complete his duties toward his employer could suffer loss of employment, poor references affecting the hope of future employment, and the financial impact of being unemployed. As these situations reflect, usually duties include both affirmative motivations (other-centeredness) and motivations arising from the fear of adverse personal consequence (self-interest).

What about life in the church? What motivates church members to consider their duty toward other church members? Why should one church member love another church member in Christ? Why should one member be concerned about the spiritual, emotional, and physical well-being of another member? When conflicts arise in the church, why should one member be concerned how another feels about the conflict and the painful consequences that conflict may inflict on the other person? It may be fear of negative consequences or it may be a more profound calling at work—the calling to consider the interests of others and not merely self-interest. Why should a Christian be motivated to even think about the concept of duty? Philippians 2:1–5 begins to address these questions.

If you have any encouragement from being united with Christ, if any comfort from his love, if any fellowship with the Spirit, if any tenderness and compassion, then make my joy complete by being like-minded, having the same love, being one in spirit and purpose. Do nothing out of selfish ambition or vain conceit, but in humility consider others better than yourselves. Each of you should look not only to your own interests, but also to the interests of others. Your attitude should be the same as that of Christ Jesus.

The apostle writing to the church's members at Philippi tells them that the reason they should fulfill their duties toward one another is the threefold motivation wrought by (1) the benefits they have personally experienced by being united with Christ and thereby united to one another as the children of God, (2) personal humility, and (3) the example of Jesus, their Lord and Savior. These sources of motivation should be sufficient to move conflicted church members toward one another in the quest for peace and unity. But there is more: "For Christ's love compels us, because we are convinced that one died for all, and therefore all died. And he died for all, that those who live should no longer live for themselves but for him who died for them and was raised again" (2 Cor. 5:14–15).

Here, again, we see the Word of God declaring that the motivation toward the performance of one's duty of care toward others in the church comes not from fear but from a unique *union with Christ* that now is to motivate and govern, indeed *"compel"* the Christian to do his or her duty to love others with humility. While this passage emphasizes our duty to live for Christ, how does Christ call us to fulfill that duty? By living for and serving others, of course. First John 1:9–10 and 1 John 3:10 make our duty toward others clear as we live out of Christ's love in us. We are called to encourage and comfort others because of our changed status in Christ.

Further, and finally, in the context of keeping one's body pure, we who call ourselves Christians are told, "You are not your own; you were bought at a price" (1 Cor. 6:19–20). If we are not our own but owned by Christ at the price he paid on the cross for our sins, then we will love others as an overflow of the love we have received from God, expressed at the cross for us. *Fulfilling one's Christian duty toward another is tied intimately to our identity in Christ.*

Since Christ did for us what we could not do for ourselves, we now have the duty and joy of doing for others what they cannot do for themselves—namely, extend other-centeredness, humility, encouragement, and comfort, even in conflict.

Church Membership Vows

Nothing in life affirms our Christian duties more explicitly and biblically than the membership vows we take when we join our local church. Are you tempted to skip this section right now because you haven't taken any membership vows or because your church doesn't even have membership vows? Please don't. Consider just a few words on how you are called to join a church as a formal member and take vows accordingly.

In an age when individualism and antiauthoritarian views dominate social life, too many people, even genuine Christians, have prioritized their own personal views over and against God's plan for life in partnership with him and his people. Many who reject God's pattern for relationship seek to justify their stand against church membership by constructing a pseudotheological argument from apparent biblical silence on the topic. But then, just like a couple that lives together outside of the bonds of marital vows and one day finds no structural support or reason to stay together when hard times come, casual church attendees find no support or reason to remain in a church body when conflicts arise.

Christian duty, as reflected in church membership, paints a very different picture of the Christian life, however. Consistently God's Word presupposes that Christians will be formally joined to a local Christian church. Some people object because the words *member* or *membership* are not used in Scripture to set forth a formal organizational tie to a local church. However, the word *Trinity* is not found in Scripture, yet all orthodox Christians believe in this doctrine. In fact many of the beliefs we share as Christians are not built on a single, specific passage or word in the Bible. Most of the doctrines derive from good and necessary inferences that God himself requires us to draw from a multitude of implicit biblical teachings. Similarly, the warrant for formal church membership does not appeal to any explicit passages for its support.

We should say, though, that the word *member* is, in fact, used in Scripture to define one's relationship to the church. Are you surprised? Consider the following passages together. "Now you are the body of Christ, and each one of you is a part of it" (1 Cor. 12:27). "We are members of his body" (Eph. 5:30). "So in Christ we who are many form one body, and each member belongs to all the others" (Rom. 12:5).

God describes our membership *in Christ* not merely in eternal terms but also in those of temporal significance. Consider Matthew 16:18 and 18:15–18, the only times Jesus used the word *church* during his earthly ministry. As such, it seems to arise out of thin air, without any precedence. Yet if this were true, we would expect to find his disciples dumbfounded, asking, "What was that word you used?" or "What's a church?" But they do not ask such questions. The implication is that they knew full well what Jesus was talking about. And indeed they did, for the concept of church is not unique to the New Testament. It takes its precedent from the Old Testament church, "the assembly of God" or "the people of God." The Old Testament church was founded on God's covenant with Abraham. The new covenant is the fulfillment of this covenant in Christ into which all believers enter (Gal. 3:6–8, 14).

Jesus sees the church in a definite way. He does not say that the church is merely a worldwide movement of believers who, when they see fit, come together for worship, prayer, and study of God's Word. In Matthew 16 Jesus says he will build his church. And in Matthew 18 he gives a very specific picture of the local church doing a very specific thing—disciplining a member for the purpose of restoring his fellowship with the body of believers, the church.

Moreover, the majority of the names used to describe Christians denote their *corporate* identity; they are in a covenant relationship with other Christians. So we are called members of the body of Christ, living stones being built into a spiritual house or temple, brothers, sisters, fathers, mothers. These all imply we are members of a special family, God's family. The pattern of the Christian life in the New Testament was always contemplated within the local body of believers. Identifiable church membership supports the kinds of relationships you would expect from those who are called to speak "the truth in love" to one another (Eph. 4:15). A vow is a promise, and a typical membership vow affirms not only one's fealty to Christ as Lord and Savior, but also to protect the peace, purity, and unity of the church. Membership vows clarify and establish our duties to Christ, his church, and one another.

A Mini Case Study

We assisted a church that was shocked to discover that an associate pastor had embezzled more than one hundred thousand dollars from the church's funds. Within a few days other church leaders sought counsel from a local attorney and were preparing to write a letter to the congregation, trying to protect the church as a corporate body. As we counseled with them, however, they began to see that such a response would not appropriately address all of the groups and individuals involved. It was hard for them to step back from a merely legally driven solution intended to protect the church's assets, but thankfully they did, because their obligations went beyond that goal.

We helped them identify various individuals and groups that the church's leaders had duties and responsibilities toward.

1. God
2. The associate pastor who confessed to the embezzlement
3. The associate pastor's family
4. The congregation as a corporate *spiritual* body
5. The congregation as a legal nonprofit corporate entity (with assets and liabilities)
6. The church officers themselves (with spiritual responsibilities and potential legal culpabilities)

In relationship to the duties and responsibilities to each of these parties, there were points of apparent conflict. Such conflicts had to be stated in the form of an issue before any potential solution could be fully considered.

Although we explained ways to protect church leaders from legal liability and preserve the financial assets of the corporate entity, we also reminded the leaders of their responsibility in ministering pastoral care to the associate pastor, his family, and other church members. If the church leaders considered only what their attorney advised from a civil and criminal perspective, they would undoubtedly choose the world's way and protect only corporation interests. Though it was the attorney's duty to protect the church as a corporate entity, the church leaders also had to consider the situation from a pastoral perspective. They were wise to seek counsel from a legal professional, but the leaders needed to make decisions that were inclusive of all of the parties and their interests, including (and most important) their spiritual interests.

Different counselors (for example, attorneys, pastors, consultants) will see a situation from various perspectives, and members of different groups will see the situation from varying perspectives too. Wisdom is never found in considering only one narrow perspective based on single issues and interests. Various perspectives should be considered, to be sure, but a perspective of one fallible human being can never be perfect and should never be determinative of next steps. Instead, all relevant individuals and groups should be considered before any reality testing of potential solutions goes forward. Otherwise a "solution" could actually lead to even more problems in the future because it addresses only one narrow perspective of the conflict.

Apply This to Your Church Conflict

Rather than closing this chapter with another case study of people "out there" in a church conflict, we thought we'd tell you an abbreviated version of how Dave's fulfilling his duties to Tara helped us both when our relationship was severely conflicted. This happened when we first started working together at Peacemaker Ministries and worshiping at the same small church in Billings, Montana.

Like all conflicts in the church, ours had elements of James 4 idolatry: Dave not only wanted but subtly *demanded* that Tara treat him with the respect due him as her elder, as a much more experienced conciliator (pastor, counselor, attorney, human); and Tara not only wanted but subtly *demanded* that Dave go along with all of her (young) enthusiastic ideas and changes, in her way and according to her timing.

130

Some of our conflicts were related to personality: Tara is effusive and choleric; Dave is more subdued and reflective. Our conflicts revealed our weaknesses. Dave's hearing disability was increasing just as Tara's rapid rate of speech was becoming even faster. Our conflicts also revealed our strengths. Tara's efficiency and effectiveness is matched by Dave's wisdom and experience. Tara may be able to hold the attention of thousands, but Dave actually has something meaningful to say. And our teaching styles are completely opposite—Dave scripts his seminars; Tara teaches improvisationally. Dave is slow and careful; Tara is fast-paced. Once, after team teaching The Peacemaker Seminar, we even received the following feedback: "Dave: Teach Tara to slow down. Tara: Teach Dave to speed up."

Truly, had we not both been bound by the fear of man (Prov. 29:25), we could have been a great team. But instead of enjoying one another and working together as a team, we began to harbor criticism and judgment against one another. This began to affect not only our working relationship but our fellowship in the church family and the fellowship of our families as well. Finally, things came to a head when Dave said to Tara in a moment of peak frustration: "You are scaring me to death!"

I (Tara) couldn't believe it! Dave? Pastor, lawyer, military leader, conciliator-extraordinaire Dave? I was scaring him? Oh, no! I saw in a flash I had totally failed in my duties toward him.

And I (Dave) knew that I was failing in my duties toward Tara as well. In that moment, we both saw with striking clarity how our relationship was a reflection of our hearts—hearts that were in desperate need of the love of Christ so we could love one another.

As Wayne Mack states, "Whenever conflict occurs, you can assume that one or both people need to come into a more vital relationship with Christ."[1] This was true of us. Thankfully, Dave remembered his duties to me (Tara), as an older brother to a younger sister, as a fellow church member to church member, as an ordained church leader to layperson, and as a fellow employee to employee. He began to counsel me with patient forbearance and abiding love. He confronted me and helped me to change. He did not require that I improve before he entered into my life. Instead, filled with the love of God in Christ, he fulfilled his Christian duty to love me as his sister and he helped me to grow up and learn how to fulfill my Christian duties to him as well. Not only did I learn how to be less threatening, but Dave grew in his confidence in Christ so that even when I failed to be gentle, he was less intimidated.

Now, with the benefit of eleven years of hindsight, we can smile as we remember how conflicted our relationship was for a season. But apart from recognizing our duties to one another, we never would have persevered through our conflicts. Things would have gotten difficult and we would have bailed. But grace enabled us to remain and grow.

Our prayer for you, as you face the conflicts in your church, is that you will remember your Christian duties. God places many responsibilities on church leaders. That is, of course, for good reason—leaders have specific duties and responsibilities related to their church leadership roles. But all members of every Christian church—including leaders—have affirmative duties of followership. This is because specific spiritual gifts have been given to each of God's people for the purpose of building his church. When leaders fail to lead in biblically faithful, authoritative ways, not only does church conflict develop, it thrives. But when both leaders and followers demonstrate proactive devotion—to the Lord, to his bride the church, and to one another—and when both leaders and followers fulfill their duties regarding their authority relationships, the beauty of the Triune God is reflected to a watching world and church conflicts are redeemed.

Questions for Reflection

1. First John 3:10 says, "This is how we know who the children of God are and who the children of the devil are: Anyone who does not do what is right is not a child of God; nor is anyone who does not love his brother." How do you think this verse relates to the concept of performing one's Christian duty in the midst of conflict?

2. In your church's present conflicts, what do you feel compelled to do? Be honest and forthright! As you consider your feelings, read 2 Corinthians 5:14–15. What changes in attitude must you make to demonstrate you are under the control of Christ? Are your duties also your delights?

3. When you joined your church what vows did you promise to keep? If no vows were taken, what would Christ expect of you as a congregant in your church? In your present conflict situation, how are you fulfilling these promises?

Recommended Resources for Further Study

Edmond P. Clowney, *The Church* (Downers Grove, IL: InterVarsity, 1995).

Mark Dever and Paul Alexander, *The Deliberate Church: Building Your Ministry on the Gospel* (Wheaton: Crossway, 2005).

Donald S. Whitney, *Spiritual Disciplines within the Church: Participating Fully in the Body of Christ* (Chicago: Moody, 1996).

10

Shepherd-Leadership

You know that those who are regarded as rulers of the Gentiles lord it over them, and their high officials exercise authority over them. Not so with you. Instead, whoever wants to become great among you must be your servant, and whoever wants to be first must be slave of all. For even the Son of Man did not come to be served, but to serve, and to give his life as a ransom for many.

Mark 10:42–45

If we're going to prevent church splits, we must be the kind of leaders who can take a hit without escalating the battle, who can diffuse issues in a godly way that actually strengthens relationships in the church. And we must be models of what it means to actively, tenaciously, intentionally, and lovingly pursue deep and wide relationships in the body of Christ.

Thabiti Anyabwile

Recently much has been written about the character, quality, and practices of a shepherd-leader. Of course, this is the only kind of leader described in Scripture as qualified to be a church leader. Unfortunately concepts of church leadership have been significantly influenced by leadership concepts from the secular world: the corporate leader, the military leader, the political leader, and the charismatic leader. The driving reason behind the church's attraction to these deviant models of church leadership is twofold:

pragmatism and familiarity. Church members requiring spiritual leadership seem to prefer a leadership model they apparently believe works and one they relate to based on their most common experience, which has been gathered, of course, from everyday secular interaction (employment, school, and other organizations).

Many Christians don't know what to do with a true shepherd-leader who uses both the staff and the rod with wisdom and proper balance. The staff is the biblical symbol for care, assistance, direction, and encouragement; and the rod is the biblical symbol for correction, discipline, orderly rule, and equity.[1] Scripture describes both of these leadership qualities and practices as a comfort: "Your rod and your staff, they comfort me" (Ps. 23:4).

How many church members do you know who are clamoring for leaders who will employ the rod and staff in biblical balance as they carry out the role of church leader? Typically followers don't make such demands on their leaders and, therefore, fail to encourage rightly balanced expectations of their church's leadership.

The scope of this book is not to educate followers or leaders about the full range and implications of biblical church leadership or biblical church followership. Many excellent resources already exist that address well these aspects of church life. (We list a number of them at the end of this chapter.) Rather, we note the most common conflicts leaders face in the church and patterns of failed leadership and failed followership that frequently define the church in conflict. We state emphatically, however, that churches in conflict will not experience an end to conflicts until they sort out and live out proper biblical roles for leaders and for followers, both of which are equally valuable in the sight of God.

Common Conflicts Involving Church Leaders

Without a doubt, many church conflicts center around church leaders. Some of the most common church conflicts involving leaders stem from the following:

- *Moral failure.* Frequently church leaders plunge their churches into conflict when they are caught in actions that are inconsistent

with their professions of faith. Church boards and congregations struggle to respond appropriately to such weaknesses in
their spiritual leaders.

- *Immaturity.* Many church leaders show their immaturity as they
  are motivated by worldly measures of success (money, title, attendance numbers, acclaim/being known) and are unwilling and
  unable to work through conflicts in a humble and redemptive
  manner. Rather than focusing on Christ and his kingdom, immature leaders focus on themselves. They can be manipulative and
  legalistic, unteachable and proud. Immature leaders are unwilling
  to be confronted, unwilling to admit weaknesses, and unwilling
  to confess sin. Limited life and ministry experience has given
  them neither hard-earned wisdom nor depth to their theology.
  Many immature leaders live within the realm of idealism.
- *Failure to meet expectations.* All church leaders have a wide
  range of expectations thrust on them. Sadly, rather than focusing on using their gifts according to Ephesians 4:11–12, many
  church leaders set themselves up for failure by trying to be all
  things to all people. Moreover, many pastors are not very effective at teaching their congregations what a biblical model
  for pastoral leadership in the church really should be. As a
  result, lay leaders and members set their own standards, and
  those standards frequently are not met because the pastor does
  not know what is expected and what conduct is considered
  the norm. Typically, complaints against church leaders revolve
  around failures to meet expectations in preaching, leadership,
  peacemaking, accountability, following through on commit-
  ments, and modeling personal piety.
- *Failure to implement change appropriately.* When mishandled
  by leaders, change in the church causes many conflicts. A pastor
  may attend a seminar or read a book and suddenly be motivated
  by a new vision for the church. The problem comes when he or
  she does not do the hard work of laying a deep biblical foundation for change that will slowly result in broad consensus and
  willing implementation.
- *Personality differences that drive sinful responses.* Of course
  people are different and sometimes those differences strengthen

a church but often they lead to conflicts, as people pick favorites and sides. Worldly responses to conflict, rather than biblical ones, are particularly prevalent when strong personalities clash.

- *People who have power and influence, even without any formal leadership position.* Some church leaders have official "positional" authority but no real power. When they conflict with people with *great* power (even though they have no official positional authority), church conflicts escalate—for example, when the chairman of the missions committee (positional power) is continually confronted by and undermined by a committee member who is also one of the largest financial donors to missions in that church. That donor has no positional power, but he wields great actual power nonetheless.

- *Using church leadership positions for self-centered reasons.* Many church conflicts reveal ways in which leaders have misappropriated church resources for their own selfish gain. God takes this very seriously and will hold selfish church leaders accountable for their sin (Jer. 22:13 and 1 Peter 5:3–4).

- *Idolatry.* Too often, church leaders place personal demands ahead of the centrality of Christ in the church. Many pastors fall into idolatry as they make the success of their ministry, rather than Christ, the center of church life.

Four Characteristics of Failed Leadership

In one church intervention I (Dave) did, the senior pastor had served for years and had an extremely close relationship with the congregation. So close was the relationship that he actually wielded significant personal control over the laypeople. Serious conflicts began to develop as new leaders came onto the church council, leaders who did not willingly submit to his control. As the pastor felt his influence over the leaders lessening, he took extreme steps to try to maintain his control over the congregation. One Sunday morning he even went so far during his sermon as to stare down everyone in the church and demand that they raise their right hand to show that they were with him. (That was the Sunday when the other church leaders met to formally approve the hiring of a mediation team to help the church.)

In contrast to that former church leader, I have also had the joy of meeting many church leaders who are true shepherds, caring for the flock entrusted to them. They strive to live in accordance with the biblical character requirements for church leaders as set forth in 1 Timothy 3 and Titus 1, and their daily lives reflect the fruit of the Spirit in Galatians 5:22–23.

Sadly, leaders in the midst of destructive church conflict rarely reflect these character traits. Instead, four characteristics of failed leadership tend to surface in the church:

- Church members learn not to expect biblically balanced shepherd-leadership.
- The leader develops a "hired hand" mentality.
- The leader no longer accepts responsibility to be an example of spiritual maturity.
- The leader no longer has a long-range vision.

Lost Shepherd-Leadership

Church members will follow church leaders whom they know will place their welfare ahead of any self-interest, ease, comfort, convenience, or control. But frequently during church conflict, members do not see balanced shepherd-leadership as Christ describes it.

> He calls his own sheep by name and leads them out. When he has brought out all his own, he goes on ahead of them, and his sheep follow him because they know his voice. But they will never follow a stranger; in fact, they will run away from him because they do not recognize a stranger's voice. . . . I am the good shepherd; I know my sheep and my sheep know me—just as the Father knows me and I know the Father—and I lay down my life for the sheep. (John 10:3–5, 14–15)

Church leaders are empowered to lead when they have followers who readily accept sacrificial leadership even when it doesn't align with personal agendas and favored opinions and preferences. The best followers are those who want the whole counsel and practices of God taught, preached, and consistently delivered, and the best leaders are the ones who do this.

A "Hired Hand" Mentality

In John 10 Jesus describes the weaknesses of the hired hand as a shepherd:

> The hired hand is not the shepherd who owns the sheep. So when he sees the wolf coming, he abandons the sheep and runs away. Then the wolf attacks the flock and scatters it. The man runs away because he is a hired hand and cares nothing for the sheep. (John 10:12–13)

Many good seminary and Bible college graduates who had the vision, idealism, and heart for pastoral ministry have fallen prey to the reality of financial survival (not wanting to risk losing their jobs) and have become, as far as their ability to lead the flock is concerned, hired hands. In their efforts to achieve a selfish agenda or serve their own sinful idols, their followers have robbed them of the freedom to be shepherd-leaders by holding the fear of unemployment over their heads.

Church leaders who leave their congregations when the church is in conflict confirm their status as mere hired hands who have no commitment to legacy vision and who have forgotten their duties to be examples.

I (Dave) observed such a failure of shepherd-leadership in a conflicted midsize church a few years ago. The pastor had left the church of his own accord several months earlier. As I attempted to draw from him his perspective on the causes of the church's conflicts and the reason he decided to leave rather abruptly, he launched into a tirade against the elders, his associate pastor, and various other members of the church. He insisted that his former sheep were evil and he had no recourse but to depart quickly.

When he finally quieted down, I asked him, "In the nine years prior to this conflict when you had preached, taught, and led this congregation, did you ever detect any rebellious spirit in the people you now clearly hate?" To my surprise he said no. Here was a man who for nine years had been in the position of trust with these sheep but

139

when the wolf attacked (when serious conflict came to the church), he ran away. My further investigation revealed signs of the hired hand: moving to distance himself from the conflict, becoming more and more an isolated and detached caretaker, leading elder meetings but avoiding decision making, not praying with anyone. He demonstrated little care for the sheep—apparently caring more about the preservation of his résumé and reputation, positioning himself to accept a call to another church without the taint of a record of conflict. This man clearly was not a shepherd-leader, as described in John 10.

Lack of Leadership Example

In Acts 15:7 we see Peter standing up to address the apostles, elders, and those who had brought doctrinal conflict to the church. Peter takes action as a shepherd-leader to confront the conflict. Of course Peter had previously failed to lead when his fear of man had caused him to be "afraid of those who belonged to the circumcision group" and he had drawn back from ministry to the Gentiles (Gal. 2:12). Many New Testament scholars (such as Dr. F. F. Bruce and Dr. D. E. Johnson) believe that Paul wrote Galatians before the apostolic council that is described in Acts 15, and therefore that the confrontation Paul describes in Galatians 2 occurred some time before the council convened. The fact that Peter now, at the council, stands up to oppose the heresy of the Judaizers is a powerful demonstration of personal change when propositional truth is embraced. Peter's "hypocrisy" (v. 13) had been challenged by Paul, and Peter had grown.

Church leaders can change by boldly and humbly embracing eternal truth over the hypocrisy wrought by the fear of man. Later we see Peter writing to "God's elect, strangers in the world, scattered throughout . . ." (1 Peter 1:1). One of the topics he addresses in this letter is the role of church leaders to be examples.

> To the elders among you, I appeal as a fellow elder, a witness of Christ's sufferings and one who also will share in the glory to be revealed: Be shepherds of God's flock that is under your care, serving as overseers—not because you must, but because you are willing,

as God wants you to be; not greedy for money, but eager to serve; not lording it over those entrusted to you, *but being examples to the flock.* (1 Peter 5:1–3)

Peter, who at the first church council stood to be an example to his fellow assembled elders, writes to all future elders (not just those first receiving this letter), appealing to them to be examples to their flock. The question naturally follows: Examples of what? This question is answered from the context of Peter's appeal: be model shepherds, provide model care, serve as model overseers, model God's interests and desires ahead of your own, be a model of willing service, a model of eager service motivated by nothing but God's glory. All this, *and* be a model of humble repentance regarding personal sin. After all, while understanding their responsibilities and callings regarding their shepherding role, all church leaders continue to be examples of sinners saved by grace (just like the sheep they lead).

No Long-Range Legacy Vision

When church leaders are in conflict, their vision tends to become very self-focused and concentrated on the present situation with little thought given to long-range vision for the church. Also they give little thought to the impact of the conflict on church members and future church leaders (even the children of the congregation). This lack of long-range "legacy vision" can facilitate church conflicts going on unrestrained for years. Deep wounds can remain for generations. All Christians, but especially church leaders, are called to have a deep and serious concern for the reputation of Christ and his church. In 1 Corinthians 6 we see one expression of Paul's concern for the church's reputation before a watching world: "But instead, one brother goes to law against another—and this in front of unbelievers!" (v. 6). Too often when the church falls into conflict, little consideration is given to the impact such conflict will have on the reputation of Christ and the church. The loss of any church's reputation in a community not only affects that church but the whole Christian family. Serious long-term damage to evangelistic outreach can result. The price of failing to consider the long-term "legacy impact" of conflict can be painfully high.

Be Prepared

In Acts 20 the apostle Paul instructs the elders of the church to take action *before* the wolves attack the flock.

> Keep watch over yourselves and all the flock of which the Holy Spirit has made you overseers. Be shepherds of the church of God, which he bought with his own blood. I know that after I leave, savage wolves will come in among you and will not spare the flock. Even from your own number men will arise and distort the truth in order to draw away disciples after them. So be on your guard! (Acts 20:28–31)

We pray that all church leaders will intentionally prepare to guard their sheep by taking steps to respond to and curtail church conflicts as the potential arises in the daily habits and practices of the local church. Even if your church is presently at peace or has a history of relative tranquility, be aware that conflict, in one form or another, is coming. But with the active and intentional ministry of church leaders, lay members and other leaders will be able to redeem their church's present and future conflicts.

Mini Case Studies

First Timothy 3 and Titus 1 set forth the character qualities required of every church leader. Titus 2 states:

> In everything set them an example by doing what is good. In your teaching show integrity, seriousness and soundness of speech that cannot be condemned, so that those who oppose you may be ashamed because they have nothing bad to say about us. (Titus 2:7–8)

Notice this call to an exemplary life as a leader directly relates to conflict. Service as a shepherd-leader is to be service characterized by one who "cannot be condemned" because nothing bad can be said about him or her—not that the person doesn't sin, but that he or she models a biblical response to sin when it occurs.

Frequently it has been said that a congregation's spiritual maturity will not exceed the maturity level of its leaders. If that is so, church leaders are to embrace their role as a personal example of holiness. Practically, what does this look like? Here the power of antithesis can help answer the question. What must a church leader *avoid* to be a legitimate example? We need not even mention obvious sin, but consider Scripture's warning regarding conflicts: "Don't have anything to do with foolish and stupid arguments, because you know they produce quarrels. And the Lord's servant must not quarrel; instead, he must be kind to everyone, able to teach, not resentful" (2 Tim. 2:23–24).

As professional mediators, we have seen few church leaders who consistently meet this standard of holy living in Christ. But those who do stand out and are worth mentioning by way of example:

- One pastor had the courage to stand before the gathered church and confess how he had sinned by making rash comments that offended some members. The result of this kind of confession was that church members placed him at a level of even greater esteem in their hearts and minds because they saw Christlike humility in action. This is modeling.
- Another pastor confronted an angry wife about her harsh treatment of her husband and had the courage to ask for her gun as she walked down a hall in her home with it pointed at him. The wife saw her pastor's courage and eventually agreed to receive additional counseling that led to a renewed marriage.
- We met a lay leader who refused to continue a discussion in an elder board meeting because it had turned to gossip about a church member who was not present. Standing up to his peers was an act of courage that called fellow elders back to the Christian standard for speech in Ephesians 4:29. Other elders from that day forward were much more careful how they spoke about others.
- An overworked pastor would regularly volunteer for nursery duty to demonstrate how Jesus's call was for every Christian to love and care for the little children, the future of the church. The result was that the church never lacked for volunteers in the nursery. If the pastor could do this, so could they.
- There was a pastor who had been at the center of great church conflict. During what he thought was to be his last sermon at

the church, he broke down and confessed his sins that had led to so much pain for the church. The result was a renewed call for him to stay on and lead everyone to a real change of heart, the same gift of repentance he had demonstrated that morning. Many said they had seen the power of humility and it changed them.

- Church leaders in one church were initially conflicted over what they wanted in a new pastor (a pastor who would be popular and likely draw large crowds; a pastor who would relieve them of the burden and accountability of decision making; a pastor who would not compromise biblical truth) but they laid before the congregation only that final option. The church today is a model of peace, purity, unity, and spiritual growth because the elders spoke with one voice and called a shepherd-leader who was equipped, ready, and willing to employ both staff and rod in ministry.

- We've seen pastors and elders of a church show up for routine workdays to clean, paint, mow, and attend to the church facility alongside the deacons and members, to encourage them and show that they were not above doing the work they desired others to do. Members fell in love with their leaders as they watched them participate alongside the common people.

- Pastors and elders in the face of vicious attacks by some of their members listened quietly to the complaints and responded with love and care. They modeled gentleness and patience even though charges were unfounded. Eventually the antagonists were silenced by the quiet calm and gentle spirit of the men they had attacked. Such gentleness shut their mouths (see Titus 2:7–8).

- Leaders in one church brought charges against an errant and abusive pastor before the ecclesiastical body that held his credentials. Such action by the leaders was without anger or revenge, even though hundreds of hours of additional work were required to follow through. These men modeled courage and love well above the call of duty and did so with a kind and gentle spirit that was truly admirable. The church was protected and defended.

All of these examples demonstrate that God is still working to conform people to his image so that the lives of God's children in the church will reflect what it means to live a life consistent with the name Christian. Leadership in the church is to be far different from the selfish and self-centered leadership so often seen in the world. Rather than seeking positions of leadership to advance personal careers or gain the praise of men, church leaders are to be servants whose only goal is the exaltation of Christ and the building up of every member so that they may mature to a life consistently lived for God's glory and honor. Praise is not sought. The goal is not self-seeking; the goal is to serve.

> You know that the rulers of the Gentiles lord it over them, and their high officials exercise authority over them. Not so with you. Instead, whoever wants to become great among you must be your servant, and whoever wants to be first must be your slave. (Matthew 20:25–27)

Apply This to Your Church Conflict

As you consider the leadership implications involved in your church's present conflicts, remember that foundational steps to prepare for, curtail, and wisely respond to church conflicts should become second nature to the daily habits and practices of the leaders of every local church. It is not enough to merely preach the Word of God; leaders are to live in accordance with the Word and help their members do likewise. The greatest failure of the church in the opening years of the twenty-first century is biblical leadership. All too often ordained and lay leaders alike fail to lead their churches with a unity of vision that will endure beyond divisive conflicts. Most church conflicts either reside in these leader groups or grow because ineffective leader actions fail to address in a timely and appropriate manner the conflicts that fester and erupt in the congregation. Leaders must lead and they must do so with intentionality and wisdom from heaven.

> Who is wise and understanding among you? Let him show it by his good life, by deeds done in the humility that comes from wisdom. But if you harbor bitter envy and selfish ambition in your hearts, do not boast about it or deny the truth. Such "wisdom" does not come

down from heaven but is earthly, unspiritual, of the devil. For where you have envy and selfish ambition, there you find disorder and every evil practice.

But the wisdom that comes from heaven is first of all pure; then peace-loving, considerate, submissive, full of mercy and good fruit, impartial and sincere. Peacemakers who sow in peace raise a harvest of righteousness. (James 3:13–18)

Questions for Reflection

1. "For you are with me; your rod and your staff, they comfort me" (Ps. 23:4). At your church how is the ministry of the "staff" being fulfilled? The ministry of the "rod"?
2. How can you gently encourage your leaders to be the shepherds that you could easily follow? How could you gently but creatively convey to your leaders that they are acting like "hired hands" who make it difficult for people to follow them?
3. What "legacy" do you think you are building through your words and actions as you deal with the church's present conflicts? What legacy would you like to build?

Recommended Resources for Further Study

Ajith Fernando, *Jesus-Driven Ministry* (Wheaton: Crossway, 2002).

Barbara Miller Juliani, ed., *The Heart of a Servant Leader: Letters from Jack Miller* (Phillipsburg, NJ: P&R Publishing, 2004).

Timothy S. Laniak, *While Shepherds Watch Their Flocks: Reflections on Biblical Leadership* (Matthews, NC: ShepherdLeader Publications, 2007).

Timothy Z. Witmer, *The Shepherd Leader: Achieving Effective Shepherding in Your Church* (Phillipsburg, NJ: P&R Publishing, 2010).

11

Biblical Followership

Remind the people to be subject to rulers and authorities, to be obedient, to be ready to do whatever is good, to slander no one, to be peaceable and considerate, and to show true humility toward all men.

Titus 3:1–2

To be part of the universal church isn't enough. . . . Every Christian is called to be passionately committed to a specific local church. Why? Because the local church is the key to spiritual health and growth for a Christian. And because as the visible "body of Christ" in the world, the local church is central to God's plan for every generation.

Joshua Harris

Every person in a local church is an officer of Christ by the mere fact of membership. Every member of a local church is a leader by the mere fact of the interaction and influence he or she has with others. Even children profoundly influence the lives of others! We lead by example. We lead by teaching. *But most of all, we lead by following.* As Old Testament scholar and renowned expert on church leadership Dr. Timothy Laniak notes: "Followership is the beginning—and end—of effective leadership."[1]

Often conflicts related to followership arise in the church because the fall (Gen. 3) has distorted our attitudes toward and our experience of authority (v. 16). When we are in authority, we are tempted to neglect our responsibility or to abuse it by lording it over others. That is part of God's curse on men as a result of Adam's and Eve's rebellion (v. 16). When we are under authority, we are tempted to servility or usurpation. These sinful responses to authority reveal our conflict with God and may lead to interpersonal conflicts as well.

A biblical response to authority structures will lead us to demonstrate "proactive devotion"[2] to our leaders. Pastors and biblical counselors Wayne Mack and David Swavely put it this way:

> Think the world of your leaders. Paul says that we should "esteem them very highly" [1 Thess. 5:13], but that translation does not even come close to representing the full meaning of the original text. "Very highly" could be translated "abundantly out of all bounds, beyond all measure" because it is a compound word that piles up three Greek prepositions for the sake of emphasis. . . . The motivation for submission, according to Paul, is not our personal feelings toward leaders, but the desire to obey God by loving them, and the realization of their position before the Lord.[3]

There is protection and even joy in following! To quote Rev. Thabiti Anyabwile:

> A healthy church member orders himself under the leaders of the congregation as a soldier orders himself in the rank and file beneath a military general. We are to joyfully, eagerly, and completely submit to our leaders for our good, their good, and the good of the entire body.[4]

Absolute Authority and Limited Authority

Everyone is under authority:

- Government authorities (Rom. 13:1–4; 1 Peter 2:13–15)
- The church and its leaders (Heb. 13:17)
- In the home (Eph. 5:22–25)
- Employers (1 Peter 2:18)

As we meet these divinely appointed authorities, we meet God's authority, for all authority is established by God (Rom. 13:1; Matt.

23:1–2), and God is sovereign over all authorities (Gen. 45:8; Dan. 2:19–22; Acts 2:22–24; 4:28). God delegates his authority to various human entities to use for his glory and as a kingdom benefit for those they lead. We submit absolutely to God because he has absolute authority, but everyone else wields delegated authority and so we submit, but not absolutely. There are limits (see Acts 4:18–20; 5:27–42). No one has the authority to command another person to sin, because God has not delegated that authority.

We are called to honor, respect, and submit to the one delegated with God's authority (Exod. 20:12; Rom. 13:1–5; Eph. 5:22; 6:1–8; Col. 3:18–25; 1 Tim. 2:1–2; 5:17; Titus 2:9–10). This is true whether we like the leader or not. Ken Sande writes:

> [We are warned] not to confuse position with personality. Even if we do not care for the way someone in authority behaves, that alone does not justify disobedience. (Imagine throwing a traffic ticket back in the face of a rude policeman—you would soon be answering to an even higher authority!) When God places people in a position of authority, He expects us to obey them unless there is a valid reason not to do so.[5]

Our natural tendency is to rebel against authority and try to justify our rebellion (even when we call it something else or it looks like something else). Quickly we insist on our way, blame our leaders, and claim legitimate grounds not to submit. Such rebellion is a serious and wicked sin (1 Sam. 15:23), because any perceived deficiencies in our leaders do not release us from our obligations to them (see Matt. 23:1–3; Acts 23:1–5; 1 Peter 2:18).

Even if a person in authority is selfish, neglectful, or overbearing, he or she is still entitled to respect! Even if a person in authority is ungrateful, should we still seek to serve and look out for his or her best interests? Yes! When we ignore these God-ordained parameters and try to do things our own way, we are showing a lack of obedience to and faith in God. God promises he will take care of the situation through proper channels or by his own divine intervention. From the world's perspective, these are all difficult and foreign ideas, but for the Christian, they define an important aspect of faith. Showing respect and trusting our church leaders is an act of submission to

God that demonstrates the depth and maturity of our faith. It is an act of trust in him that is bigger than the sins or mistakes of people, and he is indeed going to keep his promise to work all things together for our good (see Rom. 8:28).

True Submission

Years ago, we both had the joy of consulting with a Christian missionary agency regarding their conflict management policies. One of the former missionaries told of appealing a field decision to his field director, then to the national director, and finally to the international office. When all of his appeals were decided against him, he quit. That is not submission.

These were not black-and-white matters of clear-cut sin or lack of sin. These were wisdom calls, and the leaders had the authority to make them. Yes, the man had a duty to inform his leaders and to do his best to help them make the wisest decisions. But then he was called to submit. If we submit only when we agree, that's not submission. That's agreement.

In contrast to that situation, I (Dave) helped a church with a disciplinary case involving a bitter divorce situation. The husband and wife were both members of the same church. She sued him for divorce, and he responded with great anger. Actually the wife ended up leaving the church and never looked back. She moved away and never had any contact with the church leaders again. But the husband stayed. He stayed and was disciplined in a manner appropriate to the situation. Over time, he became repentant and submitted to the church's discipline. He was not excommunicated; he was barred from the communion table for a while; he was publicly rebuked before the congregation. But he stayed in the church. Initially he had taken an appeal to the governing body of his denomination because he felt a few things were unfair. The governing body upheld the actions of the elder board. Then he had a decision to make: would he continue to stay and submit or run? He stayed. Eventually he married a godly woman in the church and even became an elder. To me, he was a hero, a true spiritual giant because he submitted even when things were tough.

Sadly, he was soon after diagnosed with a fast-moving cancer. Just before he went on to glory, I wrote him a letter telling him that he was my hero. I knew how difficult the disciplinary process was. Unfortunately staying and submitting as he did is a statistically rare occurrence in the church. But his life bore beautiful fruit for several years. He helped other people with their difficult marriages; he counseled with compassion. He led by following. What made him a spiritual giant was that he stayed and submitted.

Bearing with Our Imperfect Leaders

Just as a physical head is on top of a body, a leader has headship over his or her followers. Those under authority align themselves with their leaders in such a way that they can serve their leaders and benefit from their leadership. Of course, as wonderful as headship is (and it is wonderful!), our leaders are not perfect. No matter how hard they try, their leadership will always be flawed. They may misunderstand their followers, take offense at something someone does or says, or simply not like certain personalities. In their fallenness and sin, they may actually wrong someone intentionally. The most common hurt leaders inflict on followers is neglect—leaders fail to give their followers the proactive attention and care they long for. The question is: How will you respond when your leaders let you down? And how will you help others as they interact with your leaders? All of you will remember that even when you experience disappointment with the leaders in your church, you are still called to honor God's Word: "Obey your leaders and submit to their authority" (Heb. 13:17). However, that doesn't mean that the sins or abuses of leaders should be overlooked. True shepherd-leaders submit to corrective discipline (see chap. 12).

Biblical followership means following shepherds because we realize we need a spiritual leader. Followers who are willing to help make their leaders' work as fruitful as possible demonstrate biblical followership. These followers realize that their thoughts and actions will significantly influence how their leaders lead. Just as a sheep in a flock has certain natural characteristics (a tendency to lose focus, wander away, be weak in the face of predators, and so on), so do church members. Those natural characteristics define, to an extent, what the shepherd leader is to do and how he is to lead. He must, of course, know the flock's characteristics very well to lead them at their greatest points of need and weakness.

Typically, in our churches today, we find followers who don't want to follow because they think they know more than their leader. They are like rebellious sheep who just want to do what they would do naturally. It's true that all leaders are imperfect. But we can all learn to follow imperfect leaders. We have no other choice, for there is no perfect leader in a fallen world, and as followers, this is what we are called to do.

A painful and yet beautiful example of this is a woman I (Tara) helped. Her marriage was very difficult, and her church leaders, though involved, were inexperienced in biblical counseling and biblical peacemaking. They made mistakes but they truly wanted to do what was biblically correct. Although this woman suffered greatly, she did so with great love and patience, realizing that her temporary circumstance was not just about her—it was also about helping her church leaders grow in knowledge, wisdom, and ability to serve as officers of Christ's church. Her marital and familial conflicts concerned her church family, and so she endured patiently as her church leaders stumbled, erred, and caused hurt. Yes, she wept. Yes, it was hard. But God was glorified throughout the process, and her church was strengthened as she lived by faith and modeled what it looks like to be a biblical follower. This dear woman remembered that leaders are human; leaders are in the process of growing too. They are just as much in need of grace as followers are.

A Mini Case Study

Most of the time leaders see things we can't and have information we don't. For example, I (Tara) assisted in a conflict that involved formal church discipline. Because of my position of helping the leaders and the member, I was privy to information others didn't have. I heard angry, baseless accusations against leaders from people who presumed to know all the facts but who in fact did not. The church's leaders knew things about the situation that the church's laypeople didn't and shouldn't know. The leaders could have brought forth evidence and defended themselves but to do so would have revealed information inappropriately and so they remained silent. Leaders with good processes, and especially those who have been trusted in the past, can answer concerns without revealing details. They can reassure followers that they have followed biblical processes with humble hearts and in the light of these processes have taken appropriate actions.

This case provides an excellent reminder of how important it is that we who are followers (and that's all of us!) trust our leaders and not insist that we know the details of all matters. In this day of 24/7 news and insider information, it can be tempting to force our way into what C. S. Lewis described as "the Inner Ring." We want to know more than is appropriate to know. Such nosiness leads only to gossip and factions. Christian unity is maintained and protected when we trust God and our leaders. We don't need to know everything that's going on but we can pray and look for opportunities to be a part of the solution. We must understand that many times it would be unloving and ungodly for leaders to reveal the details of sensitive church conflict matters. We can submit with joy because we know God is in control.

Apply This to Your Church Conflict

As you consider your role as a follower in your church (even if you are an ordained leader, you are also a follower), how are you affirming the gifts and strengths of your leaders, and how are you bearing with their weaknesses? Remember how gentle and patient God is toward you—that it is his kindness that "leads you toward repentance" (Rom. 2:4). How can you reflect gentleness, patience, and kindness toward your leaders? Remember, just as it is hard for you to receive their correction if they don't have a relationship with you, the same is true for them. Ask yourself if the only time you contact a leader is when you need something. Or do you and your family reach out to your leaders throughout the year to encourage them, pray for them, and bless them? Do you communicate to your leaders regularly that you appreciate them? One of the most appreciative and encouraging things you can do for your leaders is to pray for them and let them know you are doing so. This will demonstrate your proactive devotion.

Questions for Reflection

1. What is your motivation to be a biblical follower?
2. Do you struggle with authority? Romans 13:1 says in part, "There is no authority except that which God has established." If you struggle with authority, how might that be an aspect of spiritual conflict?
3. What is one thing you could do now to demonstrate your commitment to followership in your church?

Recommended Resources for Further Study

Thabiti Anyabwile, *What Is a Healthy Church Member?* (Wheaton: Crossway, 2008).

Edmund P. Clowney, *Living in Christ's Church* (Suwanee, GA: Great Commissions Publications, 1986).

Elyse Fitzpatrick and Dennis Johnson, *Counsel from the Cross: Connecting Broken People to the Love of Christ* (Wheaton: Crossway, 2009).

Joshua Harris, *Stop Dating the Church: Fall in Love with the Family of God* (Colorado Springs: Multnomah, 2004).

12

Accountability We Should Cherish

We proclaim him, admonishing and teaching everyone with all wisdom, so that we may present everyone perfect in Christ.

Colossians 1:28

Nothing is so cruel as the tenderness that consigns another to his sin. Nothing can be more compassionate than the severe rebuke that calls a brother back from the path of sin.

Dietrich Bonhoeffer

Christian churches are to enjoy the blessing of mutual accountability and redemptive discipline. The standard for accountability and discipline is, of course, the Bible (Prov. 3:11–12; Matt. 18:12–20; 1 Cor. 5:1–5; Gal. 6:1; James 5:19–20). Many solid churches with the opportunity to turn their churchwide conflicts into truly redemptive encounters fail to do so because they have failed to embrace and consistently practice redemptive, corrective church discipline. But the catch-22 is that a church cannot move in the direction of loving their people through discipline unless intentionality of ministry and fixed biblical standards have been established and consistently modeled over a significant period of time.

Those responding to the early church's conflict knew that boundaries were important and appropriate: "We have heard that some went out from us without authorization and disturbed you, troubling your minds by what they said" (Acts 15:24). The early church fathers recognized that without a meaningful authority structure in the church there would be trouble. To be meaningful, any authority structure required a means of accountability.

Church life without accountability is not really church life at all. Take, for example, the church whose deacon leader leaves his wife and small children to live with a woman from his workplace. After initiating divorce proceedings against his wife, he shows up on Sunday morning with his lover. And the church does not confront him! To see our brother caught in sin, sinking beneath the waves of the world, and to do nothing to restore him gently (Gal. 6:1) is to submit to the devil's deception. This is not demonstrating love as a family of Christ. This is not even showing concern for a stranger—for even most strangers would call 911 if they saw someone in imminent danger. How much more should we who are one body respond when someone's soul is in jeopardy of perishing?

All Christians need accountability, and thankfully a biblically faithful, love-expressing church will provide accountability that we appreciate and may even cherish.

Many biblical passages assume that Christians can identify their leaders, people to whom they are required to submit and obey and who exercise real authority over them. Moreover, Scripture equally assumes that church leaders can identify the members whom they are to watch over and for whom they will give account (Phil. 1:1; 1 Thess. 5:12; Heb. 13:17). Friends and visitors of a church are not under the authority of the church's leaders.

Accountability Structures

Throughout the Bible the church is a governed body of believers, and Paul mentions a number of accountability structures for the church. God's plan for the church brings to us the many benefits we enjoy now as we prepare for eternity:

- Communal practice of the sacraments
- Pastoral care

- A "one-anothering" community
- A witnessing community

All of these benefits are the fruit of accountability in the church. If all Christians remembered these benefits and valued them, many destructive church conflicts would be avoided. And those church conflicts that were not avoided would be more constructively resolved.

Communal Practice of the Sacraments

Former pastor and theologian Edmund Clowney once stated, "The Lord Jesus Christ addresses his church, not only in the language of Scripture, rich with the symbolism of revelation, but also through the sacramental signs he has appointed."[1] These sacramental signs are baptism and the Lord's Supper, which mark the presence and work of God and our participation in his saving grace. They are signs that accompany his declared saving Word of grace and they mark initial and continuing inclusion in God's church for those who believe.

> These outward signs mark out a visible fellowship; they structure Christ's church as a community with membership. Baptism requires a decision about admission to the community. The Supper, a sign of continuing fellowship, implies the exclusion of those who have turned away from the Lord.[2]

Furthermore, the sacraments remind us of our fellowship with one another; they are corporate blessings not celebrated in private. The sacraments are the Word made visible, joining with the preaching and teaching of the Word by which they gain their authority. Together, the communal practice of the sacraments and hearing the Word support the claim that God's grace is ministered to us within the formal membership and fellowship of the church, Christ's body. First Corinthians 10:17: "Because there is one loaf, we, who are many, are one body, for we all partake of the one loaf." People who have not publicly professed their faith in Jesus Christ are not invited to participate in communion. Likewise, Christians who need to be reconciled to fellow Christians are urged to "first go and be reconciled" (Matt. 5:23–24) prior to taking communion.

Pastoral Care

Hebrews 13:17 states: "Obey your leaders and submit to their authority. They keep watch over you as men who must give an account. Obey them so that their work will be a joy, not a burden, for that would be of no advantage to you." Some of the work of our elders/overseers is to prepare us "for works of service, so that the body of Christ may be built up" (Eph. 4:12), and to ensure that we recognize and turn away from sin whenever it takes us captive (Matt. 18:17–20; Gal. 6:1; 2 Tim. 2:24–26). A specific example of pastoral care, "so that the sinful nature may be destroyed and his spirit saved" (1 Cor. 5:5), is commanded by the apostle Paul as he guides the early church in its spiritual care responsibilities. It takes maturity to appreciate the benefits of church discipline, but who would not want all the help they can get to live a life worthy of the calling they have received in Christ (see Eph. 4:1)?

As the parable of the lost sheep (Matt. 18:10–14) makes clear, every one of God's children is dearly loved and worthy of being reclaimed when he or she falls into unrepented sin. Unrepented and unconfessed sin divides us from God's fellowship and the fellowship of the other members of Christ's body. Being among those identified and identifiable means enjoying the pastoral care of those called and ordained to the task of rescuing lost sheep.

A "One-Anothering" Community

The Scriptures list some fifty-five ways Christians are to be specifically serving each other within the church. Church members enjoy the priority of the administration of God's grace through the exercise of spiritual gifts given to members of God's family (see 1 Peter 4:10). This priority is particularly spoken of in Galatians 6:10: "Let us do good . . . especially to those who belong to the family of believers." Besides the command to "love one another" (1 John 3:11), we are to be doing everything from greeting one another (1 Peter 5:14) to bearing one another's burdens (Gal. 6:2). What a joy and privilege it is to receive the ministry God has for us as well as to minister to our brothers and sisters using the gifts he has poured out through the Spirit!

Meaningful accountability in the church means far more than just the privilege of voting at a congregational meeting. For instance, only members should have the privilege and responsibility of teaching Sunday school classes, serving in the nursery, serving as ushers and church officers, and using their individual spiritual gifts to minister to one another. When people accept Jesus as Lord and Savior, and after joining a local church, they use the spiritual gifts God has given them to build his church.

A Witnessing Community

The Bible teaches that God's wisdom is to be revealed through the church. This revealed wisdom includes knowledge of his plan of salvation in Christ for all humankind, including the rulers and authorities in the heavenly realms (Eph. 3:10). The church, therefore, is God's witnessing plan. We faithfully follow the plan of the Great Commission when we baptize (include) people into the church and when we teach people to obey everything Christ has commanded (Matt. 28:19–20). Christ commands that his church be built in accordance with his plan, with the oversight of church leaders who are accountable to him (Matt. 16:18–19; Heb. 13:17). Also we follow the Great Commission's plan when we demonstrate our love for the eternal souls of Christian brothers and sisters by seeking to rescue rebellious believers who refuse to repent of sin (see 1 Cor. 5:5). Both acts, *inclusion* and—when appropriate and required—*exclusion*, define the witnessing community of the church.

Of course, not many conflicts arise over *inclusion* in the church. Most of the time that is a celebratory season of extending the right hand of fellowship when making and receiving membership vows. In many cases, however, conflicts escalate when churches attempt to disciple their members with real *accountability*—especially accountability leading to *exclusion*.

One term for these steps of discipleship is *church discipline*. Church discipline is a means of God's grace in our lives. Without it, we would probably just fall away from the church and become apostate if ever blinded by the deceitfulness of sin or tempted to unbelief by Satan or the world. But under the umbrella of protection of our local church authority, we know that there are church leaders

159

who are committed to our rescue. They will leave the ninety-nine other church members and seek us out if we wander away (Matt. 18:12–14). They will run to the side of the boat, call for help, and even jump in the water at their own peril to keep our heads above water if they see us caught in sin and sinking under the weight of our own spiritual rebellion (Gal. 6:1–2).

Such selfless, loving, and courageous acts are the heartbeat of church discipline. But it's sad that today many churches do not rescue their lost lambs or drowning members. It is heartbreaking for Christian parents to watch their teenagers and young adult children leave their homes and wander away from the church. If a young mother abandons her husband and children or a man leaves the wife of his youth after forty years of marriage, these are tragedies indeed. But many churches just stand back, allow the relational wreckage to happen, and then do their best to pick up the shattered pieces after the crash.

We believe that there is something much better: *the faithful exercising of the authority that Christ places in the hands of the local church*. This begins with "the care of friends," to quote Edmund Clowney—friends who love us enough to tell us the truth and to *get help* if we are caught in sin or unbelief and we refuse to repent. They may reach out to other wise and spiritually mature friends or to an ordained church leader. But the most important thing is that true friends will not see us in mortal, spiritual danger and just shake their heads and say, "Oh. Too bad." No! True friends will rally the resources of the entire church, if necessary, to rescue us! And if we remain hardened in our hearts, if we are caught up in loving our sin more than our Savior, if we are acting like a nonbeliever, then our church leaders will love us enough to *formally* discipline us.

This formal discipline is sometimes called *judicial* or *corrective discipline* because the church is sitting as a court and ruling (through their tears) and saying: "This person is acting so much like a nonbeliever that we are going to treat her as a nonbeliever. This means that she cannot participate in certain things that are only for Christians: taking the Lord's Supper, for example, or teaching a Sunday school class. This does *not* mean, however, that we will shun her or despise her or avoid her. Oh, no! Our love for her will only press in stronger and deeper. But whereas we used to interact with her as a fellow believer, we will now interact with her as a *person to be evangelized*. Just as we remind one another of our great need of the gospel of Jesus Christ, we will faithfully remind her of her great need of the gospel of Jesus Christ and we will urge her to repent—to come back to the Lord, to return to the church, to come back to the fold. This is church discipline.

And both Dave and I have had the heartbreaking (initially) and happy (when restoration occurs) experience of helping churches with this restorative, protective, loving process. Let us share with you just two examples.

I (Dave) assisted a group of church leaders who were disciplining a man for his unethical business practices. Initially this man was furious. He had no interest in discussing his financial and business dealings with the church leaders. But the leaders insisted because every less formal attempt (through wise and caring friends in the church) had failed.

First of all the leaders gave this man every opportunity to express his perspective on the situation. He had a fair and open hearing during which even he began to see how some of his actions were not glorifying to the Lord. As the details of how he cheated vendors a little bit here and failed to pay his bills on time there came out, the Holy Spirit was already at work convicting his heart.

It took a lot of time and effort by one elder and one deacon in particular as they met with this man regularly to study the Scriptures regarding how a Christian businessman ought to behave, but it was worth it. By the end of the formal discipline process, this man was repentant. Not only did he begin to pay back the money he had wrongfully withheld from vendors, he even offered to pay the money back with interest to make up for his wrong. Not only were the fruits of his repentance seen in his business and the protection of the reputation of Christ's church, but his marriage benefited as well! His wife told the leaders how much happier and less stressed he was at home, how he began to read the Bible more, and that he even had more patience with their children. God was at work! This man was rescued and renewed.

I (Tara) participated in the church discipline process of a young man who was physically abusing his wife. My role was not as an ordained church leader, but as a helper called in to assist the church leaders when the young wife called them for help from the emergency room. They did not want her to meet with an elder alone and when they asked whom she would like to have present, she asked for me. As I sat next to this frightened, bruised young woman and the church leader explained how another church leader was down at the police station to be present for her husband's arrest and booking, I remember thinking, *This is church discipline. It is middle-of-the-night, 24/7 availability to help a member of the church.*

Yes, she was the victim and she needed special protection and care, but the young man had grown up in this church and he was a member. He, too, needed special help—help from men who were bigger and stronger than he; help from the criminal justice system as well; *help to wake him up and encourage change.*

Edmund Clowney captures perfectly the biblical truth of these examples.

> The gifts of others encourage us when we despair, minister to us in sickness, and remind us of the faithful promises of God. They also warn and rebuke us, even declaring God's condemnation of our sin. Discipline is essential to the pursuit of holiness. God himself chastises us as children and he uses fellow-Christians to hold us responsible to our common Master.
>
> Discipline . . . is not first an exercise of negative judgment, a matter of church courts and censures. It begins with the care of friends with whom we strive to follow Christ, and to whom we are, in a measure, accountable. We now sometimes use "disciple" as a transitive verb, which is how the Greek word is used in the Great Commission. But Christians are Christ's disciples, not ours. We serve others as we minister the truth and love of Christ.[3]

Abuses of Church Discipline

Of course we assume that many of you reading these lovely examples of church discipline may be struggling a bit because you are thinking of a number of *unlovely* examples of church discipline. Perhaps you have seen church discipline in the form of harsh and arbitrary treatment at the hands of mean-spirited men and women bent on punishment or revenge. We have too. Many of the conflicted churches that finally reach out to conciliators for assistance do so because of huge conflicts related to the unfair, uneven, biased application of church authority. Please know that any time church discipline is exercised in such a destructive way, it is not discipline at all. In fact it might rightly be described as abuse.

What do abuses of church authority look like? Consider just a few examples:

- The leader saying, "Obey ME!" (rather than obey God).
- There is an ongoing air of secrecy and fear.
- Leaders do not listen to counsel and are accountable to no one.
- Other "leaders" go along with everything the abusive, authoritarian leader wants. People are afraid to confront the leader in any way.
- There is no Christian liberty; matters of preference and wisdom are made into law (required), and conformity to the law/requirement is coerced (either subtly or overtly).
- The atmosphere is one of deception and double standards.

We could go on and on because there are so many other examples of abuses. But when seen in antithesis to the good news of God's abiding love and care for his children through the accountability and discipline of the church, any abuses become the black velvet against which the sparkle of his diamonds shine more brilliantly. Therefore, we *urge you* to study this topic further and consider what God's Word has to say about how the church is to function regarding accountability and discipline. Dr. Clowney, in his excellent book, *The Church*, states:

> Three marks were defined in distinguishing a true church of Christ: true preaching of the Word; proper observance of the sacraments; and the faithful exercise of church discipline. . . .
> If the church is identified by the Word and the sacraments, church discipline uses the keys of the kingdom to maintain that identity.[4]

Consider the fact that the only recorded instances when Jesus used the word we translate "church" during his earthly ministry are both in the context of accountability (Matt. 16:18–19; 18:17–20).

In the same way, 1 Corinthians 5 clearly reveals that Jesus intends his church to be built on the regular use of that authority by church members and leaders. No one can deny that these passages are in the Scriptures, yet many churches act as if they are not. In the context of church conflict it is rare to find the faithful practice of account-ability. Yet ironically, many devastating church conflicts would be avoided or dealt with much faster and much more redemptively if accountability (discipline) were faithfully and lovingly administered. In fact in all of the cases of church conflict we have worked with, the greatest failure of the church has been to ignore the full counsel of God by failing to practice biblical, redemptive, corrective church discipline. Until that changes, churches will continue to struggle with the devastation of conflict, and the ministry of the gospel to the entire world will be impeded. In the words of Jonathan Leeman: "Insofar as the Gospel presents the world with the most vivid picture of God's love, and insofar as church membership and discipline are implications of the Gospel, local church membership and discipline in fact define God's love for the world."[5]

If the church really desires to be faithful, and if it really desires to resolve its conflicts in a manner that builds the church and its members' faith, then an understanding of God's love as expansive enough to include discipline will follow. Until that day, however, the church will continue to be crippled, underutilizing all that is so readily available to it.

(Lack of) Mini Case Studies

God's Word, when faithfully applied, can change the course and out-come of difficult church conflicts. We know this is true, but sadly, in all of our years serving as Christian mediators, we know of very few case studies in which church leaders faithfully practiced redemptive, corrective church discipline and followers submitted to church account-ability. Ideally we would have many such stories of how a person, once confronted through the faithful practice of corrective measures, and shown the depth of his or her rebelliousness, would come to his or her senses, repent, and the course of the church's conflict would be dra-matically altered. But many church leaders fail to wield the authority of the keys of the kingdom to attempt correction of their members. And many times, if members are confronted, they promptly run away.

The entire culture of the church is in need of renewal so that when any God-ordained practice is employed, a Christian under the jurisdiction of the church does not merely flee as an unbeliever and outcast. We can think of no greater challenge for the church today. We can think of no greater need than to teach Christians what it means to make a vow to God to be a part of his church and then to welcome as a benefit of that membership the reality of accountability and love through redemptive church discipline. This includes *formative discipline*—the work of the church wrought through preaching, teaching, and fellowship (see Acts 2:42–47)—and it means, when necessary, *corrective discipline*—the intervention, through the exercise of the church's authority, to educate us about the danger of our unrepented sin and its outcome so that we will turn back to the right path.

Apply This to Your Church Conflict

First Corinthians 5 talks about an accountability that you should cherish. On the day of the Lord, if you've appropriately held a person accountable for his sin, his soul will be saved. This is the bigger purpose for the church. This is a bigger perspective of the church. And truly, isn't this one of the very reasons that your church exists—*the salvation of souls*?

As you reflect on these biblical truths and strive to apply them to your church's conflicts, we pray that you will not give in to worldly, negative views of accountability and church discipline. As you remember the *benefits* of accountability and church discipline and the *responsibilities* of accountability and church discipline, you will see a path to the redemption of your church conflicts.

Questions for Reflection

1. Why should you "cherish" personal accountability over those things you say or do that are inconsistent with the faith you profess?

2. Does your church practice redemptive, corrective church discipline as an act of pastoral care? How do you think this tool that Jesus says he will use to build his church (see Matt. 16:17–19) could be used in your church to redeem its present conflicts?

3. How has God's work of "formative discipline" prepared you to accept and cherish "corrective discipline"?

Recommended Resources for Further Study

Mark Dever, *Nine Marks of a Healthy Church* (Wheaton: Crossway, 2000).

Kevin DeYoung and Ted Kluck, *Why We Love the Church: In Praise of Institutions and Organized Religion* (Chicago: Moody, 2009).

Jonathan Leeman, *The Church and the Surprising Offense of God's Love: Reintroducing the Doctrines of Church Membership and Discipline* (Wheaton: Crossway, 2010).

Tullian Tchividjian, *Surprised by Grace: God's Relentless Pursuit of Rebels* (Wheaton: Crossway, 2010).

Biblical Response

ACTS 15:11, 16–18

If you love me, you will obey what I command.

John 14:15

Scripture makes it clear that those who are unable to *apply* God's Word do not *truly* understand it.

John Frame

B y this point in the church intervention process, thankfully, most of the people at LCC were considering their desired outcomes in the light and glow of the powerful effect of shared eternal values. This change in perspective made a tremendous difference, and their discussions reflected a level of discernment that had been lacking early in the church's conflicts. Now with leaders and followers united in purpose, they continued to work through the biblical peacemaking principles, some of which they had already addressed.

1. *How can we glorify God at LCC?* Together, they decided that they were called to please and honor God by making top priority all of the implications of the Great Commission (proclaiming the gospel and teaching people to obey God's Word). They

knew by living out the first and second greatest commandments through faithful caregiving to all of God's people (both in the church and those presently outside of the church), they had changed their perspective.

2. *How have I contributed to the conflicts at LCC?* Individuals confessed bitterness, gossip, and slander. Children confessed their failures to honor their parents, and parents confessed how they had been exasperating their children. Leaders asked for forgiveness for putting personal preferences ahead of God's glory and the unity of his church. Members and leaders alike confessed their "fight and flight" responses to conflict, and many specific confessions were made regarding angry words and actions that had been taken.

3. *How are we called to speak the truth to one another?* As has already been mentioned, laypeople at LCC gently confronted one another and, when necessary, got help from ordained leaders. Ordained leaders were patient and faithful to try to rescue any wayward sheep. Whereas once complaints were made behind the backs of others and behind closed doors, the members and leaders at LCC now understood that they were called to speak *to* one another, not *about* one another.

4. *What does it look like for us to forgive one another just as in Christ we have been forgiven?* Oh, the reconciliations among all of the remaining members of LCC were sweet, but the family reconciliations were the sweetest! No longer did cousins have to awkwardly avoid one another because their parents or grandparents were at odds. Sunday afternoon meals were again happy and united. And when anyone involved in the conflicts was tempted to despair over the past, he or she was lovingly reminded that those sins were covered over, remembered no more.

More likely than not, just as was the situation at LCC, the ways a church responds to conflict are never officially voted on or recorded in the minutes of a congregational meeting. A pattern of response develops over years of unwritten rules subtly being handed down from one person to the next. They might sound something like this:

- "Conflict? Not us. We never disagree publicly (even if we are bitterly divided and exasperated to the point of causing a church split or simply walking out the back door)."
- "We lose a lot of people every year to unrepented sin, divorce, and conflicted relationships. But we get new people coming in so it's really just a wash. People are going to leave no matter what."
- "Poor leadership is the cause of many of our problems, but our leaders think they are above criticism and feedback, so we never talk with them; we only talk about them behind their backs."
- "I know what the Bible says, but my lawyer told me . . ."

These responses are common in our churches, even though many Christians—even Christians in conflict—would probably say that their desire is to "be biblical." Why the contradiction? Because many of us do not know what the Bible says about how to respond to conflict, and even if we *know* what the Bible says, we find it hard to *obey*.

- When do we confront?
- When do we overlook?
- Should we keep this conflict private or involve others?
- What does it mean to forgive just as in Christ we have been forgiven?
- Do we really have to love our *enemies*?

To respond biblically to these questions and live consistently with the theology we confess (see Mark 12:30), we must first understand a systematic and biblically based theology of conflict resolution. Ken Sande has developed and presented just such a Christ-centered, biblically faithful theology for peacemaking in his book *The Peacemaker*. This section does not attempt to restate all of the wisdom you will find in Peacemaker Ministries' resources. Instead, our goal is to highlight just a few of the most salient peacemaking principles applicable to church conflict and encourage you to *mine Scripture* regarding these issues.

As Christian mediators who have been trained by Peacemaker Ministries, we intervene in conflicted churches (or businesses, marriages, parachurch ministries, and families) only if everyone involved will mutually agree that "the Holy Scriptures shall be the supreme authority governing every aspect of the conciliation process."[1] It is our sincere prayer that you too will put all of your confidence and trust in the sufficient and authoritative Word of God.

We further pray that all of us will *obey* God's Word. As Jesus says in John 14:15, 21: "If you love me, you will obey what I command. . . . Whoever has my commands and obeys them, he is the one who loves me."

It is one thing to claim to love Jesus. It is another thing to obey his Word. The great battle of the ages is to live consistently with what we believe and profess. Danish philosopher Søren Kierkegaard noted: "It is so difficult to believe because it is so difficult to obey." When we respond biblically to our church conflicts, we are linking our belief with consistent actions (obedience) and thus showing our love for Jesus.

The Slippery Slope of Conflict

As mentioned at the beginning of this book, the Peacemaker Ministries' Slippery Slope depicts the range of human response to conflict. The segments on the left, Escape Responses, identify what we may do to get away from taking responsibility for conflict: first, deny there is conflict or minimize its significance; second, flee—that is, run away or otherwise refuse to deal with the situation; and third, if the circumstances are extreme, resort to the ultimate form of flight, take one's own life.

On the opposite side, the Attack Responses identify what we often do to intimidate or manipulate an opponent to abandon his or her position: assault, which is usually by verbal means but at times actual physical attack; litigate, intimidate through legal means; and, if an extreme situation, take an opponent's life.

The center six segments are the biblical alternatives to escaping or attacking and can be referred to as the "work it out" strategies or peacemaking responses. The three segments to the left of center are *personal peacemaking responses* (only my opponent and I need be involved), and the three to the right are *assisted peacemaking responses* (other Christians become involved). In church conflicts it is not unusual for the full range of these six biblical peacemaking responses to come into play.

The Four Gs of Peacemaking

Peacemaker Ministries describes a biblical response to conflict as The Four Gs of Peacemaking, and we have structured the final four chapters of this book around these essential biblical responses to conflict:

- *Glorify God.* How can I please and honor God in this situation?
- *Get the log out of your eye.* How can I show Jesus's work in me by taking responsibility for my contribution to this conflict?
- *Gently restore.* How can I lovingly serve others by helping them take responsibility for their contribution to this conflict?
- *Go and be reconciled.* How can I demonstrate the forgiveness of God and encourage a reasonable solution to this conflict?[2]

We are called to glorify God in our church's conflicts (we deal with this in chapter 13). Rather than thinking first of self, we are to seek first to please and honor God. If every Christian in a conflicted church would simply follow this one principle, redeeming the church's conflict would be well on its way.

Regardless of what other people do or fail to do, we are called to get the log out of our own eye by taking responsibility for our contributions to conflict (see chapter 14). How have we fueled the flames of our church's conflict? Actual attitudes, words, and actions may spring readily to mind. But what about sins of omission? How have we failed in purposeful love? How little have we prayed for the people involved in our church's conflicts? *What* have we prayed for them? Are we living as hypocrites—claiming to love God while hating our brother (see 1 John 4:19–21)? Repentance and confession are painful, but freeing. We can take this step toward sincere love—love without mask or pretense—because God, in Christ, has already counted us righteous.

If it is not appropriate to graciously overlook (unilaterally forgive) certain actions and attitudes of others, we may be called to go to the other person and speak the truth in love (chapter 15). This may be in private or in public. Often in church conflicts, it is a combination of the two—we keep things as private as possible for as long as possible, but at some point love for God and love for neighbor may compel us to involve others to help in the reconciliation process.

Peacemaking is hard work and frequently unpleasant. It takes faith and effort to live for God's glory with an eternal perspective. It is never enjoyable to confess our own sins and it can be terribly difficult to confront other people. But this fourth G of peacemaking—to forgive as the Lord forgave you (Eph. 4:32)—can be simultaneously one of the most excruciatingly painful experiences and one of the most exquisitely sweet foretastes of heaven that we get to experience in this life (this is the subject of chapter 16). To lavishly, freely, restoratively forgive someone in our church who has shamed us, belittled us, betrayed us, or attacked us takes a supernatural move of the Holy Spirit and reflects Christ to a watching world.

Resolving Not Just *Redeeming* Church Conflict

The foundation for all of these biblical responses to church conflict is, of course, the grace of the Lord Jesus Christ—the gospel. As we remember the gospel (Acts 15:11), we are called to live consistently with it (vv. 16–18). Christians are called to be doers of the Word

(James 1:22). For Christians in conflicted churches, this means that we are to glorify God, even in our conflicts. Personal reconciliation is possible through repentance, confession, and forgiveness. Material problems and solutions are to be evaluated on the basis of whether they are biblically legitimate (that is, consistent with Scripture) or merely based on opinions, preferences, or human (worldly) desires. If Christians involved in church conflicts would subject their personal preferences to the nonnegotiable, propositional truth of Holy Scripture, and agree that the Bible is their standard for evaluating the range of possible responses and solutions, church conflicts would not only be *redeemed*, they would be *resolved*.

Does it surprise you to hear us say that? Up to this point we have only talked about redeeming church conflicts as growing in grace and conformity to Christ, regardless of whether the material conflicts in your church are ever resolved. But destructive church conflicts are not good. In addition to redeeming your church's conflicts—which you can do regardless of how others respond—we want to actually resolve them.

For the sake of Christ's reputation in the world, God calls on us to do everything we can to bring a definite end to our church's conflicts. There is no room for compromise in Paul's words: "Therefore, if you have disputes about such matters, appoint as judges even men of little account in the church! I say this to shame you. Is it possible that there is nobody among you wise enough to judge a dispute between believers?" (1 Cor. 6:4–5).

A church's leaders and members alike have the responsibility to do all they can to resolve their material differences finally and decisively, while ending their relational strife as well. Unless the goal from the outset is clearly to bring final resolution, a church can become enmeshed in unending controversy that poisons the culture of the church for years and perhaps even decades. But as you remember and apply everything we have written up to this point, you will have a strong foundation for responding biblically to your church's conflicts and *resolving* them.

Having remembered the gospel (Acts 15:11), and looking again to the Scriptures (Amos is quoted in vv. 16–18), the church's early leaders wrote a letter to the Gentile believers stating a clear response to the doctrinal conflict that shook the early church. That letter, verses

23–29, was a biblical response containing an affirmation: "It seemed good to the Holy Spirit and to us" (v. 28). Here were the leaders of the then known church taking responsibility, applying what they knew to be true, and decisively declaring God's Word. The conflict was resolved, not just redeemed. When the people of the church in Antioch read it, they "were glad for its encouraging message" (v. 31).

13

How Can I Glorify God in This Mess?

This is to my Father's glory, that you bear much fruit, showing your-selves to be my disciples.

John 15:8

Instead of focusing on our own desires or dwelling on what others may do, we will rejoice in the Lord and bring him praise by depending on his forgiveness, wisdom, power, and love, as we seek to faithfully obey his commands and maintain a loving, merciful, and forgiving attitude.

The Peacemaker's Pledge

Often Christians in conflicted churches ask many questions:

- How can I make that person *stop doing that*?
- What is it going to take for them to see this *my way*?
- If I stop giving my money to the church, how long will it be before they shape up and *get rid of that guy*?

But such questions miss the most important question of all: How can I please and honor the Lord in my church's present conflicts? Redeeming and resolving church conflicts requires every person in-volved to focus initially not on success (winning) but on glorifying God. Such a focus leads to questions such as these:

- How can we all, as fellow church members, resolve this conflict in a way that we all can see in each other God's image with greater clarity?
- How can we demonstrate to each other that our relationships in Christ are vastly more important than winning this fight?
- How can we be part of God's successful resolution of our conflict by humbling ourselves to ask the best questions about how our sin and passion-driven desires have blinded us to the point of engaging in group conflict?

We glorify God by trusting and obeying him in church conflict. Such responses reflect right worship of the Triune God. Only right worship of God allows us to see ourselves rightly (that we are more like the other people in this church conflict than unlike them); and only right worship can displace wrong worship—*the adultery*—present in church conflicts (James 4:4). Apart from right worship, we will love something or someone more than God as temporal concerns triumph over the unseen concerns of faith. Apart from right worship, we will willingly sacrifice other people on the altar of desires—money, property, worship styles, ministry leaders, "winning this fight," "being right," or "getting my way." Only right worship can effectively foster deep and lasting *heart and attitude changes* that prioritize the value of eternal grace above the things of the world.

Acting on Our Beliefs

Glorifying God in church conflict means going beyond belief to actually acting on those beliefs. God doesn't leave us speculating about how we are to glorify him when confronted with conflict in the church. For example, in Matthew 18:15–20 several specific steps are to be taken to confront a fellow Christian with his sin, steps that call increasingly for broader church involvement. Or see Matthew 5:23–24, where we are specifically told what to do and when to do it if we learn that someone has something against us. Romans 12, 1 Corinthians 5, and Galatians 6 are other examples of God's clear direction when it comes to the task of resolving conflict.

So why do so many Christians fail to obey these Scriptures? Because belief is only half the story. The other half is the actual doing—putting belief into action. In the words of noted pastor and author Rev. Dr. Paul Tripp, "Spiritual maturity results from practicing truth in everyday life, not knowing truth in one's mind."[1]

In Matthew 15:8–9 Jesus quotes the prophet Isaiah: "This people honors me with their lips, but their heart is far from me; in vain do they worship me, teaching as doctrines the commandments of men" (ESV), or, as the New International Version renders it: "They worship me in vain; their teachings are but rules taught by men." In too many churches today, we see extremes. Some churches look and sound so like the world that they are indistinguishable from non-churches; other churches are so alien from society that their forms and rituals have grown cold, distant, and irrelevant. Both extremes are far from what the Scriptures tell us is the heart and life of true religion: "Religion that God our Father accepts as pure and faultless is this: to look after orphans and widows in their distress and to keep oneself from being polluted by the world" (James 1:27).

A damaging church conflict I (Dave) worked with several years ago provides an excellent example of failing to glorify God when conflicts arise. The church was solid, with wonderful worship, clear biblical preaching, dynamic adult and youth educational ministries, and many focused programs geared to connecting people to the church and each other. Conflict developed when a commercial business dispute arose that involved one of the church's elders (the business owner) and the adult son of another elder who was an employee of this business. Eventually this "little" business dispute, one apparently unrelated directly to the church and its ministries, resulted in two pastors leaving the church (one leaving ministry entirely), several elders resigning their offices and leaving the church with their families, and about 25 percent of the remaining congregation forsaking their membership vows and walking away. This had been a church of about four hundred members before the conflict exploded.

These were well-educated, upper-middle-class, urban Americans and all long-standing church members. So why did conflict decimate this church? Simply stated, some members and leaders were more focused on temporary matters than on glorifying God. Commercial business interests trumped spiritual life, and the life-changing meaning and goal of God's grace in Christ meant less than immediate temporal business interests.

In addition, leaders failed to take actions in a timely manner that would have connected all of the implications of a gospel-grounded life to the words and actions being taken by many of the church's officers and members. In short, Christian belief did not influence behavior toward godliness or Christlikeness. The church did not feel called to glorify God. Yes, the people all knew the gospel message intellectually, and they knew many things about the Bible. But ultimately that knowledge was ineffective in changing how many people responded to the costly and difficult circumstances of church conflict. The people suffered. The reputation of Christ suffered. And the witness of all Christians in this community grew a bit dimmer.

Second Peter 1:3–8 addresses the connection between knowledge of God on the one hand and living a life of virtue, self-control, perseverance, and godliness on the other. Verses 5 and 6 speak to the matter of knowledge alone being unfruitful—it must be joined with faith, goodness, self-control, perseverance, and godliness to become effective. *Church leaders and church members should not expect to be able to glorify God in their church's conflicts if they have not been taught nor become practiced in making the connection between the beliefs they profess and the behaviors they exhibit in every venue of life.*

Heavenly Wisdom Rather than Worldly "Wisdom"

Glorifying God in church conflict means intentionally choosing heavenly wisdom over worldly "wisdom" (James 3:13–18). It is sad that, when conflict comes to the church, all too often the practices of the world come with it. Some people "vote with their feet" and angrily leave (an escape response to conflict). Others respond with their pocketbook, withholding financial support until the manipulative power of money brings the result they want (an attack response to conflict).

James 3:13–18 contrasts the wisdom of the world with the wisdom of God. This passage says that one is "earthly, unspiritual, of the devil," and that the other is "pure . . . peace-loving, considerate." To glorify God in your church's conflict, your calling as a Christian is to embrace wisdom that comes from God. That includes relational patterns that are pure and peace-loving rather than earthly and unspiritual, full of envy and strife ("selfish ambition"). Every Christian seeking to honor God and display his wisdom will look for intentional ways to conform to God's Word.

Of course, merely teaching people what they are to do (a to-do list from Scripture) will never actually enable them to do those things or have those attitudes. Therefore, calls to obedience, to do our duty, must always be rooted in a declaration of God's saving achievement in Christ and nourished by the means of grace.

Glorify God by Suffering Well

Finally, Christians are called to suffer well as they glorify God in church conflict. The biblical doctrine of Christian suffering stands out on the pages of Scripture. Romans 8:16–17 is one of those central passages that tie the expectation of our suffering with the suffering of Christ: "The Spirit himself testifies with our spirit that we are God's children. Now if we are children, then we are heirs—heirs of God and co-heirs with Christ, if indeed we share in his sufferings in order that we may also share in his glory."

Suffering, to one degree or another, is an inevitable aspect of church conflict. When people lose treasured relationships, they experience significant loss. But suffering in the midst of a church conflict requires an examination of the difficult question: Why does one suffer in conflict?

Scripture distinguishes between suffering that is endured for Christ's sake and that which is borne by one who deserves to suffer because of his sin. First Peter 2:19–20 states:

> For it is commendable if a man bears up under the pain of unjust suffering because he is conscious of God. But how is it to your credit if you receive a beating for doing wrong and endure it? But if you suffer for doing good and you endure it, this is commendable before God.

While the context for these verses is the suffering of a slave at the hands of a master, the biblical principle applies to other situations as well. Many people suffer as a result of their own folly. For example, Proverbs 19:15 says, "The shiftless man goes hungry," and in verse 19 we read: "A hot-tempered man must pay the penalty." Usually people who expect to "win" in church conflict complain how much they suffer at the hands of those not giving in to their demands.

One woman I (Dave) met in a conflict situation complained loudly that her great suffering was at the hands of "Satan's servants"—that was the term she used to describe her fellow church members who disagreed with her. She believed her suffering was for Christ. In reality, her suffering was because of her greed. She wanted to see church resources used for things she thought worthy: new carpets, cushions for the pews, a crystal chandelier for the foyer, and also "saved for the rainy days that are sure to come." The reasons for her suffering were "unworthy" and illegitimate, yet she was convinced she suffered as a result of her love for Christ and his church. She fled the church in pain when she saw she would not win. There is no reasoning with people who cling to their idols and therefore distort or pervert a true view of suffering.

Instead, we are called to turn back to a renewed understanding of God's agenda for his children. God's sole agenda for us is his glory as we grow in holiness, and frequently this growth is a result of suffering unjustly for his sake. God's agenda for his eternal children is not merely a life of comfort, ease, or pleasure. He is fully willing to compromise all of these for the sake of our spiritual growth, so that we will grow up (that is, mature) in Christ (Eph. 4:15) and thus live for his glory.

Of course not all suffering is a result of the Lord's chastisement—it is difficult to discern what is of the Lord's origin or merely from imperfect people. We should be wary if someone pronounces that the Lord's chastisement is the source of our suffering. At such times suffering for doing good should be at the forefront of our hearts and minds. Worthy suffering results, as does the true work of the Lord's discipline, in "a harvest of righteousness and peace" (Heb. 12:11; see also 1 Peter 3:11, citing Ps. 34). If peace is not the result of our enduring trials for Christ's sake, we can be certain something else is at work. That should give us fair warning to be especially watchful in the context of church conflicts where personal agendas can easily be opposing God's agenda. Only by remembering his holy agenda can we make right decisions about our responses at such difficult times.

> To this you were called, because Christ suffered for you, leaving you an example, that you should follow in his steps. "He committed no sin, and no deceit was found in his mouth" [he did not deserve such treatment]. When they hurled their insults at him, he did not retaliate; when he suffered, he made no threats. Instead, he entrusted himself to him who judges justly. (1 Peter 2:21–23)

In the words of Jack Miller (pastor, author, and founder of World Harvest Mission):

> Life is inescapably a way of pain. The only question finally is where we seek our comfort. If we seek our comfort in the Father of our Lord Jesus Christ, then we will know joy and fulfillment beyond anything we have ever imagined. In the darkness a plan will begin to emerge. The plan must not be rushed, but it will come.[2]

A Mini Case Study

In one church conflict that I (Dave) served, I pointed out to the elders, near the end of the consulting engagement, that the pastor, who was at the center of the conflict, would have a relatively short window of opportunity in which to demonstrate that he had made the changes he had committed to during the mediation process. They understood as did the pastor that the clock was ticking. During the following months it became evident that the pastor was not keeping his promises and following through with his agreement. He was back in old patterns that were definitely hurting the church and hindering ministry. The elders prepared the pastor for the inevitable—his termination—and he agreed.

During the prior months, a single, middle-aged woman (we will call her Joyce) who was a new Christian began attending the church. Joyce knew nothing of the conflicts the church had experienced prior to her attendance. She enjoyed the pastor's sermons and thought him personable and engaging. But the day came when the elders and pastor stood together before the congregation to announce that the pastor was leaving and the search for a new pastor would soon begin. Joyce was confused and her confusion quickly turned to outrage. This was her first church, and now it appeared to her that ruthless elders were firing her pastor without adequate cause.

Joyce made a terrible scene when, with great anger, she confronted the elders after the service. Later one of the elders told me that she said, "This is exactly what is wrong with religion, people making harsh judgments and forgetting about the love that Jesus is supposed to be all about. I will never attend this or any other church ever again." And she drove off, never to be seen again.

Joyce had no context within which to understand the reasons her pastor, her only pastor, was being asked to leave. She would not listen to any explanations the elders tried to provide, would not allow any follow-up visits, and would not return phone messages. She decided to hate the church and Christianity because of this experience.

Joyce responded to the consequences of a church conflict with a flight response. Those new to the church are most susceptible to following a flight response since they have little spiritual maturity as well as little investment in the church. Those who attack are usually the long-time members or regular attendees who have been invested in the church for years. After giving a great amount of time, treasure, and relationship, many people have a strong sense of entitlement and commitment. Thus, when they don't get what they want, they feel they have earned the right to protest.

Church conflicts have this double-edged nature affecting both new and old members in the church. The best way not to endanger people is to teach them at the outset of church conflict that God is not surprised when conflict occurs and that he is teaching everyone something. In other words, each person is taught to embrace the conflict as an opportunity to glorify God and grow in grace by trusting and obeying him. People without an understanding of God's sovereign nature, however, will resist this message. But spiritually mature people who are grounded in biblical truth will understand the full implications of the gospel for their lives. They will fulfill their Christian duties to one another and will help to address church conflict redemptively for God's glory and the church's coming of age in Christ. They will demonstrate patience and grace even in the face of suffering.

Apply This to Your Church Conflict

Glorifying God by redeeming your church conflict will require you to connect the beliefs you profess with the behaviors you exhibit while you walk through your church's present conflict. It takes effort, sacrifice, suffering, obedience, faith, and love, but you can begin to teach, learn, and practice faithful obedience to Christ our Savior, even as the conflict rages. You can live for his glory, bearing his fruit, as you focus on eternity to come. "This is to my Father's glory, that you bear much fruit, showing yourselves to be my disciples" (John 15:8).

The fruit that we bear in glorifying God is eternal. His children are sanctified. The gospel is proclaimed and modeled. And, in fact, people will give their lives to Christ during a conflict if the church is being faithful to Scripture. Does that sound strange to your ear, that your church's conflicts could actually *help* your church grow as you evangelize your community? It's true! Each year my (Tara's) church uses the vacation Bible school curriculum Peacemaker Clubs.[3] We never have to worry that we won't have children in attendance because the VBS pretty much sells itself: "Hi! My name is Tara Barthel and our church is putting on a vacation Bible school about peacemaking. Tell me . . . do your kids ever fight?"

Conflict is a part of everyone's life and we can grow personally, our church can grow corporately, and our ministry can be more effective as we glorify God in conflict. Through conflict the church has a strategic opportunity to lead people to Christ, but most churches miss this opportunity, or as Dr. Alfred Poirier, author of *The Peacemaking Pastor*, states: "The Christian church lacks credibility in its witness to Christ when it displays to the world its impotence in resolving conflicts."[4]

Conflict is a unique time when people are open to really hearing the gospel because they are seeing how their false gods (possessions, career or ministry success, entertainment, etc.) fail to satisfy. Church conflicts can lead to the life-changing events that spiritually mature individual members will mold into the future of ministry for a more faithful and biblically true witness.

Questions for Reflection

1. In Ephesians 4:13 the two concepts of unity and spiritual maturity are linked together. How do you think *disunity* in the church may indicate *immaturity*? In your church conflict what spiritual immaturity is clearly evident? What can you do to help move people in the direction of maturity in Christ?
2. Hebrews 11:1 defines *faith* as "being sure of what we hope for and certain of what we do not see." In your church's present conflicts, what are you hoping for that you cannot see?
3. What is the spiritual fruit (John 15:8) that you would like to bring forth in this conflict (that is, what fruit would you like to personally demonstrate and what fruit would you like to foster in others)?

Recommended Resources for Further Study

Tara Barthel and Judy Dabler, *Peacemaking Women: Biblical Hope for Resolving Conflict* (Grand Rapids: Baker, 2005).

Alfred Poirier, *The Peacemaking Pastor* (Grand Rapids: Baker, 2006).

Ken Sande, *The Peacemaker: A Biblical Guide to Resolving Personal Conflict*, 3rd ed. (Grand Rapids: Baker, 2004).

Ken Sande and Kevin Johnson, *The Peacemaker: Student Edition* (Grand Rapids: Baker, 2008).

14

Owning My Contribution to Conflict

Confess your sins to each other.

· James 5:16

Instead of blaming others for a conflict or resisting correction, we will trust in God's mercy and take responsibility for our own contribution to conflicts—confessing our sins to those we have wronged, asking God to help us change any attitudes and habits that lead to conflict, and seeking to repair any harm we have caused.

The Peacemaker's Pledge

O f all of the problems in a severely conflicted church, one of the most devastating is the common habit we have of refusing to admit when we are wrong. There are many reasons for our being slow to confess. Sometimes we measure out blame on some sort of scale, and after determining that the other person is "more wrong," we somehow think our behavior is excused. At other times we might be willing to confess if the other person confesses first.

But Matthew 7:5 calls us to a different response, encouraging us to get the log out of our own eye. We must ask ourselves: *How have I contributed to my church's present conflicts and how can I show Jesus's redemptive work in me by taking responsibility for my wrongs?* Taking responsibility for our part in our church's conflict is particularly important if we are tempted to claim neutrality (see more on this later in this chapter). For truly, every Christian has been called to be a peacemaker (Matt. 5:9) and to "keep the unity of the Spirit through the bond of peace" (Eph. 4:3). This means that in church conflicts every member is either part of the solution or part of the problem.

Belief in the gospel of Jesus Christ changes a person's motivation and attitude. This change is characterized by a shift away from self-interest toward a greater concern for the interests of others in order to promote the interests of God. With that shift, our natural desire for self-protection through defensiveness, self-righteousness, and the desire to always be right disappears little by little as we mature.

Confession Is Good

Although it may be humbling and difficult, confessing our contribution to our church's conflicts is actually a good thing. Confession puts the gospel on display as we once again verbalize the truth that we are sinners, trusting the remedy of our great Savior. Often our reticence to confess exposes our unbelief—either we don't believe the Bible's assessment of our weaknesses or we don't functionally trust the efficacy of the sacrifice of Christ. But godly repentance and confession restore our relationship with God and others. This helps others know they are not alone in their sins and failures. Furthermore, it demonstrates faith, character, and spiritual maturity, all elements of redeeming conflict for God's glory. In the words of Rev. Dr. James Thompson:

> There can never be a genuine Christian fellowship until we can accept ourselves and each other as sinners. Where this is the case we no longer have to hold ourselves up in the presence of others, knowing that this is the one community which will accept us despite our failures.[1]

Especially as we come to the communion table, we are called to remember that it is a table of accountability that follows confession. Jesus paid the penalty in his body for our sins that we may build his church in relationships of meaningful accountability. His sacrifice means our slavery to sin has been broken. We have been set free in Christ from sin's bondage through repentance, confession, and forgiveness and can now turn again to him and to one another. In 1 Corinthians 11, when this sacred meal was being instituted, we find these words in verses 27–29:

> Therefore, whoever eats the bread or drinks the cup of the Lord in an unworthy manner will be guilty of sinning against the body and blood of the Lord. A man ought to examine himself before he eats of the bread and drinks of the cup. For anyone who eats and drinks without recognizing the body of the Lord eats and drinks judgment on himself.

If we can't confess our sin and turn from it, we must love our sin more than we love Jesus. He is the One who calls us to humility before coming to this feast, confessing to God and confessing to that fellow sheep we have sinned against.

David Powlison's "X-Ray Questions"[2] are some of the best tools you can use to identify where you may need to make confession related to your church's conflicts:

- What do you love, want, desire, crave, long for, and wish?
- Where do you bank your hopes? What are you building your life around? What do you fear?
- Where do you find refuge, safety, comfort, and escape? When you are fearful, discouraged, and upset, where do you run? Do you run to God for comfort and safety or to something else?
- In what do you trust? Do you functionally rest in the Lord? Find your sense of well-being in his presence and promises? Or do you manipulate and control and protect and try to provide for yourself?
- What makes you feel rich, secure, and prosperous? What would bring you the greatest pleasure? Misery?
- What do you feel entitled to? What do you feel is your right to expect, seek, require, or demand?
- What do you pray for? What do you think about most often?
- In what ways do you live as a slave to the Devil? Where are you susceptible to his lies? Where is your life an example of the apparent powerlessness of the Gospel?

If your responses to any of these questions reveal that your love, adoration, and worship are fixed on anything or anyone other than God, then that is what you need to confess.

The Myth of Neutrality

The myth of neutrality is common in church conflicts and can keep us from the honest examination that leads to confession. Have you fallen prey to this myth? Do you try to tell yourself that you're not involved in your church's conflicts, that you are neutral? Careful! If you are not purposefully a part of the solution, that means you are very likely a part of the problem.

We may try to claim neutrality in a church conflict, but our actual neutrality is highly unlikely, for even if we try to rationalize our so-called neutrality as a viable position, if we are aware of conflicts in our church, then we *are* involved. Our lack of engagement is actually a form of engagement—we are choosing to avoid the conflict.

In addition, most people feel strongly about their church. We may try to say, "This conflict has nothing to do with me," but, even subconsciously, we may be contributing to the poison of the conflict by our attitude, words, and actions. In private conversations with our closest friends or spouse, we may unintentionally reveal our genuine concerns about the situation: "I don't think the church leaders should be . . ." "Can you believe that she is . . . " Rather than being biblical and going to church leaders or to the person we are criticizing behind his or her back, we may be developing an attitude based on piecemeal information, hearsay, gossip, and a limited perspective. Or we may be failing to love people well by giving them the charitable benefit, as described in 1 Corinthians 13:7. We may be sitting on the fence, staying in the background, and watching our church implode around us. But the truth is, if we are trying to convince ourselves that we are not a part of the problem, we are just deceiving ourselves.

As we serve conflicted churches as mediators, a typical church member clinging to the myth of neutrality will say something like this: "I know about this conflict in our church. It makes me sad and a bit angry that we are spending so much time on it. I know people on both sides but I'm not getting involved. We should just forgive and forget and move on. Don't you agree?"

At this point in the conversation we are sometimes tempted to begin a passionate monologue about the sin of alleged neutrality when it comes to spiritual matters. Thankfully, with time and experience, we have learned to anticipate that many people will plead neutrality and try to convince us that loveless apathy is the wise response to church conflict. We have learned we can hold our emotions in check and simply teach early and often in the conflict intervention process that all members are involved in some way. We say, "If you are a member of this conflicted church, you have a choice to make. You are either part of the solution or part of the problem. There can be no fence-sitting. Avoidance may feel better in the short term, but it will never help any of the people involved to grow in grace and it will never help to resolve any of the material issues."

Most people claiming neutrality don't like to hear this counsel. Still, we persevere because they need the call to affirmative Christian duty when fellow brothers and sisters in Christ are in conflict with each other. Their membership vows compel them to not sit idly by as their church struggles. They need strong biblical guidance that teaches them unequivocally that neutrality is impossible in relation to spiritual things and that conflict in the church is a spiritual thing. Furthermore, neutrality indicates passivity in a society that is to be dynamic, involved, and caring for one another. Membership in a church demands sincere involvement in the lives of other members. Certainly there may be times when a church member should trust that their elders know more about the situation than they do and pray for the elders to deal with it wisely. Such an action is recognizing the authority that elders possess, and showing submission to that shepherding authority is a form of becoming involved. But such submission should never be used as an excuse for not becoming personally engaged with your brothers and sisters in the pews when that may be appropriate.

The Bible condemns spiritual neutrality and requires Christians to take a stand for truth. When conflict develops in the church, every member is called to the duty of being a peacemaker by "making every effort to keep the unity of the Spirit through the bond of peace" (Eph. 4:3). Fulfilling this call leaves no Christian on the sidelines.

Consider these other Bible passages: "Anyone, then, who knows the good he ought to do and doesn't do it, sins" (James 4:17). "Because of the increase of wickedness, the love of most will grow cold" (Matt. 24:12). And to the church of Laodicea, the Lord says, "I know your deeds, that you are neither cold nor hot. I wish you were either one or the other! So, because you are lukewarm—neither hot nor cold—I am about to spit you out of my mouth" (Rev. 3:15–16). Being "lukewarm" toward your church's conflicts reflects an attitude of neutrality that the Lord eschews.

Few of the seemingly well-intentioned Christians we have met who plead neutrality realize the depth of their spiritual immaturity. Similarly, others may protest by saying they don't know what to do to fulfill their calling to be engaged in their church's conflicts and be part of the solution. Pleading ignorance can be a convenient excuse but that is all it is, a mere excuse to deny the call to Christian duty. Galatians 6:1–2 makes it perfectly clear that every Christian owes every other Christian the duty of rescuing them from sin: "Brothers, if someone is caught in a sin, you who are spiritual should restore him gently. But watch yourself, or you also may be tempted. Carry each other's burdens, and in this way you will fulfill the law of Christ."

The "law of Christ" includes loving one's neighbor and loving one's enemy as well (see Matt. 5:43–45 and Rom. 12:20–21). So if you are one of those who are tempted to stay on the sidelines during your church's conflict, we'd like to encourage you to get involved as a peacemaker and give it your all. God can use you mightily; being a peacemaker isn't optional. If you've sinfully shirked your duties, confess and enjoy fulfilling your role as a member of the body.

Confession

There is really no such thing as a bad confession. A bad confession—one that tries to shift the blame and make excuses, or one that is defensive and fails to take personal responsibility—is simply *no confession at all*. It may appear to be a great confession but amounts to no confession. You can try to use the language of confession, but it is a nonconfession if it fails to reveal actual sorrow for sin.

Nonconfession is called hardness of heart. Hardness of heart leads to attempts to explain and rationalize. It does not lead to change, which is the evidence of a real confession.

A tool to help us with our confessions is the Peacemaker Ministries' "Seven As of Confession."[3]

- Address everyone involved.
- Avoid *if*, *but*, and *maybe*.
- Admit specifically.
- Acknowledge the hurt.
- Accept the consequences.
- Alter your behavior.
- Ask for forgiveness.

The Seven As help us know the parameters of a meaningful Christian confession. If we use this guideline, it becomes blatantly obvious during church conflicts when people use words sounding like confession but merely reveal a nonconfession. As some people try to deny, hide, flee, or cover up their contributions, the Seven As will help others make complete, meaningful confessions.

Groups may also need to make confessions, especially leader groups. Sometimes confessions are made in private. In church conflicts, they are often public, before the assembled church body, because without public confession, the church family will continue to be damaged by the conflict, which is public. The following story illustrates when a confession by church leaders would have been appropriate because of their failure to properly shepherd their flock and confront blatant sin.

I (Tara) saw the need for a public confession when a woman in my church left her husband to marry a man in our church she had been having an affair with. This was extraordinarily confusing to members. Does sin not matter? Are marriage vows really for life? Can I just follow in this woman's steps and do what makes me feel momentarily happier in life, or do I actually have to obey God's Word? If I get caught in sin, will anyone help me, confront me, and rescue me? What about her husband and child?

Personal unrepented sin affects the corporate body when leaders fail to confront it and call people to confess. The Holy Spirit is quenched (1 Thess. 5:19) and the ministerial effectiveness of the church is impacted. Not only was a confession called for from the adulterous man, but because church leaders failed to confront, they too sinned and their confession was needed to bring healing to this church. The *Seven A's* can guide group confession just as they guide personal confession.

A Mini Case Study: Your Confession Helps Others

In addition to experiencing the blessings of obedience, when we take responsibility for our contribution to our church's conflict and make a complete confession, we are also encouraging others to be responsible for their contributions to the conflict. I (Dave) saw this truth at work in one of the most memorable church interventions of my career as a Christian conciliator.

The presenting issue that brought us to this small southern church was a conflict between a senior pastor and an associate pastor. They had extremely divergent philosophies of ministry and within just two years of the associate pastor's arrival, the two men stopped praying together and were barely speaking to each other.

We met with these pastors for an extended, multiday mediation, and eventually the senior pastor came to the point of heartfelt conviction. He began to repent and confess his sins to the younger man. He confessed that his actions and attitudes were driven by fear. He was afraid of the younger man's energy, charisma, and how the church was growing primarily due to younger couples who were attracted to the energy of the younger man. The senior pastor saw how the church had grown more in just two years with this younger man present than in the entire fourteen years the older man had been there on his own. Fears of being compared unfavorably with this younger man drove the senior pastor deep into a dark tunnel of seemingly inescapable fear, and he became defensive. Rather than being humble and teachable in his leadership, he had tolerated no criticism or even discussion of his positional power, his sermons, or every decision, which he always considered had been right. Rather than enjoying and delighting in God's ministry through the younger man, he interpreted every success of the younger pastor as proof that his ministry and even his life had been a failure.

All of these details came out in our private mediation. After the senior pastor confessed these things, there was a wonderful reunion between the two men. This private confession brought great healing to their relationship. But there still needed to be a public confession. How does a senior pastor confess to his congregation that his ministry has deteriorated because of his fear and sin? What would be the likely result? I really had no idea. But I could encourage him to trust in the Lord as his guardian as he moved forward. I assured him, regardless of how the congregation responded to his confession, that his life and ministry would be forever changed by the insights and discernment he gained from this conflict. "Confess to your sheep," I exhorted him.

The following Sunday I stood on the platform between these two pastors. The conflict had spread through a lot of gossip and now the gossip had informed people of what was to happen that morning. There was standing room only. Like gawkers at a traffic accident, people who hadn't darkened the church door in years arrived early and packed the church to the edges. Many people thought there would be a big blowup and end with the announcement that someone was resigning or being fired.

Instead, the associate pastor confessed how he had contributed to an environment of personal strife, competition, and jealousy. It was powerful. You could have heard a pin drop. And then the senior pastor told about his fear. He confessed his complete loss of perspective of being first and foremost a shepherd to his people (including his duty to shepherd his young associate). He even told a poignant story of how he saw that pitchfork of fear in the hands of Satan just prodding him in the wrong direction, away from everything he had committed his life to as a shepherd overseer. His fear drove his sinful choices, which had led to the formation of various factions in the church. Lifelong friends were angry with each other; even families were being torn apart. He confessed his role in all of this. The associate pastor confessed his role. And then these two men literally walked right around me and embraced each other. The whole place began to melt.

I turned to the congregation and said, "You've seen your pastors model confession in true humility. Now it is time for you to go to those with whom you have broken fellowship. Confess, repent, and be healed." And they did! There was a rumbling and then a movement of people like a wave—walking across the sanctuary, looking for people to talk to. More than twelve hundred people were speaking to each other for the first time in months, confessing, receiving confessions, granting forgiveness, weeping, embracing—twelve hundred people. It went on for some time and then I asked the organist to play some music and bring them back together with a hymn. The people settled down, and the senior pastor gave an abbreviated sermon on how God uses such circumstances in our lives to grow us in grace. Talk about redeeming and resolving church conflict!

Honesty really is the best policy and honest confession, regardless of the results, is always the best avenue, because God knows what he is doing and he is clear about what it takes to overcome the deceitfulness of sin. "He mocks proud mockers but gives grace to the humble" (Prov. 3:34).

Apply This to Your Church Conflict

As you consider how God might be calling you to get the log out of your own eye and make a godly confession related to your church conflict, think about the words of Pastor Ray Stedman in his book *Body Life*:

> Nothing could be more destructive to Christian koinonia than the common practice today of pretending not to have any problems. It is often true that Christian homes may be filled with bickering, squabbling, angry tantrums, even bodily attacks of one member of the family against another, and yet not one word of this is breathed to anyone else and the impression is carefully cultivated before other Christians that this is an ideal Christian family with no problems of any serious consequence to be worked out. To make matters even worse, this kind of conspiracy of silence is regarded as the Christian thing to do, and the hypocrisy it presents to others (not to mention how it appears to individual members of the family) is considered to be part of the family's "witness" to the world.[4]

194

We all struggle. We all fail. But there is grace for the day! We don't have to be defensive. We don't have to hide. There is a way out—the way of confession and faith.

Questions for Reflection

1. Why is it so difficult to say, "I was [or am] wrong"?
2. Have you ever made a confession knowing it was only a half-hearted effort? What do you think God thought of that? What role might "fear of man" have played in the situation?
3. There is teaching in 1 Peter 5:5–7 on humility. In verse 5 Peter refers to Proverbs 3:34 and says, "God opposes the proud but gives grace to the humble." What is one certain way to experience the gift of God's grace in conflict? Why?

Recommended Resources for Further Study

Jerry Bridges, *Respectable Sins: Confronting the Sins We Tolerate* (Colorado Springs: NavPress, 2007).

Bryan Chapell, *Holiness by Grace: Delighting in the Joy That Is Our Strength* (Wheaton: Crossway, 2003).

Ted Kober, *Confession and Forgiveness: Professing Faith as Ambassadors of Reconciliation* (St. Louis: Concordia, 2002).

15

Speaking the Truth in Love

All Scripture is God-breathed and is useful for teaching, rebuking, correcting and training in righteousness, so that the man of God may be thoroughly equipped for every good work.

2 Timothy 3:16–17

Instead of pretending that conflict doesn't exist or talking about others behind their backs, we will overlook minor offenses or we will talk personally and graciously with those whose offenses seem too serious to overlook, seeking to restore them rather than condemn them. When a conflict with a Christian brother or sister cannot be resolved in private, we will ask others in the body of Christ to help us settle the matter in a biblical manner.

The Peacemaker's Pledge

Confrontation is a word with negative connotations in our culture. Biblically, however, it is not negative; it is a word of caring—going beyond the superficial to address the eternally important aspects of our growth and the growth of our siblings in Christ.

Confrontation could be direct: "Let a righteous man strike me—it is a kindness; let him rebuke me—it is oil on my head. My head will not refuse it" (Ps. 141:5). "Rebuke a wise man and he will love you" (Prov. 9:8).

More commonly in the Bible, confrontation is gentle, involving counseling, advising, instructing, appealing, warning, encouraging, and correcting. The church is filled with those gifted to help us see our blind spots. Such care-filled confrontation reflects the truth of Romans 15:14: "I myself am convinced, my brothers, that you yourselves are full of goodness, complete in knowledge and competent to instruct one another."

Redemptive confrontation—speaking truth in love—means that we are motivated by two concerns: *love of God* and *love of neighbor*. Yes, we can appropriately consider our own interests (Phil. 2:4), but first we consider the interests of others, and preeminently we are to be motivated by Christ's interests that too frequently are forgotten (Phil. 2:21). Speaking the truth must be done in love, for the ultimate good of the one being confronted and for the glory of God (1 Cor. 10:31), or else it is not redemptive confrontation.

When Your Brother or Sister Sins against You

Throughout history, telling the church that a brother or sister in Christ has become hardened in sin and refuses to repent has proven a difficult task. Today in our culture of tolerance, obeying Christ and utilizing the authority of the church to deter and turn our friends from a path of sin to a path of repentance continues to be both difficult and rare.

As already described in chapter 12, many Christians either hate the concept of church discipline or feel it inappropriate for our culture today. But church discipline is simply one way that Christians are called to speak truth in love to one another. The call of Matthew 18 and 1 Corinthians 5 to discipline redemptively is one of the greatest confirmations of God's loving care and concern for each of his eternal children. Like a loving parent, God calls his children to turn away from destructive sin and he does so by instructing his church exactly how he will use other believers in the lives of those who have become trapped in the hardness of their hearts, trapped in their unrepented sin, taken captive by the Evil One (2 Tim. 2:26).

Nowhere in Scripture do we see a greater expression of the Lord's shepherding love for his flock than we see in the church's patient practice of redemptive, corrective church discipline. The church has a responsibility to teach all of God's Word in a manner consistent with the whole message of the gospel. This includes Matthew 18:15–17:

> If your brother sins against you, go and show him his fault, just between the two of you. If he listens to you, you have won your brother over. But if he will not listen, take one or two others along, so that "every matter may be established by the testimony of two or three witnesses." If he refuses to listen to them, tell it to the church; and if he refuses to listen even to the church, treat him as you would a pagan or a tax collector.

The challenge presented by Matthew 18:17 has become almost intolerable to those who have defined the church as a loose association of people "experiencing Jesus" together by enjoying warm fellowship, music, and entertaining speakers. If enjoyment and welcoming are the primary considerations for a church, then personal accountability for sin is not usually high on the priority list.

There are numerous barriers to the faithful practice of Matthew 18:17. Fear of man, even for biblical church leaders, is a real deterrent. In addition, church leaders can be personally sued for telling the church details of a dispute! Churches that fail to obtain the informed consent of their membership and fail to regularly teach an expectation for personal accountability run the real risk of litigation for defamation of character if the church is informed.

Even with these risks, we believe that Scripture requires the local church to be the forum for resolving all conflicts and disputes between professing members as discussed below.

A Peacemaking Forum

The thesis that the church should be a peacemaking forum is logically inferred from 1 Corinthians 6:1–8:

> If any of you has a dispute with another, dare he take it before the ungodly for judgment instead of before the saints? Do you not know that the saints will judge the world? And if you are to judge the world, are you not competent to judge trivial cases? Do you not

know that we will judge angels? How much more the things of this life! Therefore, if you have disputes about such matters, appoint as judges even men of little account in the church! I say this to shame you. Is it possible that there is nobody among you wise enough to judge a dispute between believers? But instead, one brother goes to law against another—and this in front of unbelievers!

The very fact that you have lawsuits among you means you have been completely defeated already. Why not rather be wronged? Why not rather be cheated? Instead, you yourselves cheat and do wrong, and you do this to your brothers.

The language that we find in 1 Corinthians 6:1–8 arises from the context of the preceding chapter where Paul has found it necessary to admonish a particular local church, the members of which know the person involved in sin and the details of the situation, for not appropriately exercising its right and responsibility to discipline a member. Verses 12 and 13 of chapter 5 make it clear that Paul considers the church the authority to make such judgments: "What business is it of mine to judge those outside the church? Are you not to judge those inside? God will judge those outside. 'Expel the wicked man from among you.'"

Then Paul uses strong mocking language of condemnation to demonstrate the absurdity of Christians going before unbelievers to have their disputes resolved. He uses such language to shame the church. Unfortunately such a strong and urgent message is exactly what many churches need to bring them to their senses. The local church has a serious responsibility to exercise the jurisdiction that God has assigned to it. Failure to exercise that jurisdiction—by failing to be prepared as a viable forum for Christian conflict resolution—results in great shame to the church and to the church's head, the Lord Jesus Christ.

Anyone who has ever redemptively confronted another person knows how difficult it can be. In many instances, however, when shown their sin, Christians repent and change. Christians truly under conviction of their own sin become reasonable again. They come to their senses (2 Tim. 2:26). They look for new ways to understand better the positions of those they have been fighting against. They try to direct discussions back to what would please and honor God in the situation and not be satisfied with easy answers just to be done with it all. They realize with new zeal that no issue at the center of a conflict outweighs God's call to put relationships in Christ above all other considerations.

The two greatest commandments that Jesus teaches (Matt. 22:36–40) are commandments directed at relationships. And we all know that relationships take time and great effort. Real relationships are not built quickly or on a foundation of anything less than honesty and truth. Redeeming and resolving church conflicts means understanding and capturing the Lord's priority for relationships—first for a relationship with him and second for real relationships with each other. And that means "speaking the truth in love" (Eph. 4:15). According to authors Wayne Mack and David Swavely, "Whether a church practices public confrontation is an issue of obedience or disobedience to Christ. . . . A church that neglects these commands of Christ is no better than a church that neglects preaching or the ordinances."[1] (See Jesus's words against allowing sin to remain in the church in Rev. 2:14–16, 20–23.)

Means and Methods for Speaking the Truth in Love

The process described in Matthew 18:15–20—what we call "church discipline"—is actually God's search-and-rescue plan for seeking to restore a brother or sister lost in his or her sin. The steps in this passage guide us in responding appropriately to someone, based on the nature of their sin and their spiritual readiness to respond.

According to verse 15, the person most affected by the sin should initiate a personal, private discussion with the offender. Slowly the process progresses to include others if, and only if, the offender being confronted is unwilling to listen, turn from sin, and repent.

If the offender immediately repents and confesses, no one else needs to be involved or even hear about the situation. The matter is finished if his or her confession is genuine and if the person stops sinning and makes every effort to change as well as make whatever restitution is necessary to the one he or she has wronged. If the person has sinned against others, he or she needs to demonstrate repentance and confess sins to them as well. Only in the case when the offender refuses to listen—that is, if he or she fails to acknowledge sin and the need to repent, confess, and receive forgiveness—would the person who was wronged proceed to the next steps.

Matthew 18 is so important to our understanding of how to redemptively confront a person that we'd like to lead you through an extended analysis of the chapter. We will begin by backing up to the start of the chapter to see the context. Chapter 18 is the fourth of five blocks of discourse, alternating with blocks of narrative, and it begins with the disciples asking Jesus a question: "Who is the greatest in the kingdom of heaven?" (v. 11). We know from several other passages that this question was frequently on the mind of the disciples (see Luke 22:24). This is a question driven by human pride, self-centered righteousness, and a craving to be considered the best.

We must grasp that this self-centered, desire-driven attitude is at the heart of the disciples' question in Matthew 18:1 to understand the full extent and context of our Lord's reply. First, he calls a child into their midst and says, "Unless you change and become *like* little children [that is, totally dependent], you will never enter the kingdom of heaven. Therefore, whoever humbles himself *like* this child is the greatest in the kingdom of heaven" (vv. 3–4). We emphasize the word *like* because it demonstrates that Jesus's teaching here goes beyond those present at the moment. Using the word *like* makes it clear that Jesus is teaching all of us, as God's eternal children, that we are called to change if we are to see the kingdom. We are called to exalt humility over our idolatrous passions and desires, whatever they may be.

And then Jesus turns to the topic of sin. "If anyone causes one of these little ones who believe in me to sin, it would be better for him to have a large millstone hung around his neck and to be drowned in the depths of the sea" (v. 6). Whoever is at the center of sin in the church, causing others to be a part of sin, is in grave peril.

The church (all leaders and members) are called to do the work of speaking the truth in love by calling back those who have fallen into unrepented sin. After speaking of the dreaded awfulness of sin, Jesus tells the disciples this parable, the immediate context for the passage most closely associated with the church's practice of discipline. Verses 12–14 say:

What do you think? If a man owns a hundred sheep, and one of them wanders away, will he not leave the ninety-nine on the hills and go to look for the one that wandered off? And if he finds it, I tell you the truth, he is happier about that one sheep than about the ninety-nine that did not wander off. In the same way your Father in heaven is not willing that any of these little ones should be lost.

The members of the church are referred to as "these little ones." This is not a parable about reaching those outside of the fold. The context is that of the little child, the one who has placed his trust for eternal life in Jesus, who has humbled himself, who has without reservation believed. It is also in the context of sheep, the term the Bible uses repeatedly to refer to those who are the Lord's (see John 10:27 and Ezek. 34).

The rescue of a believer trapped in sin is at the very heart of the whole message of the gospel. When someone has placed his trust in Christ and has professed that faith publicly in joining the church, he or she has become part of God's flock, God's family. A special relationship has formed—a bond—and the church is called on in a special way to be there whenever one of its members is in danger, especially when sin has taken him or her captive.

If we understand that this parable is directed toward believers who need rescuing from sin, it should be a great comfort to us. Jesus uses it to convince us that when a beloved believer, one of his flock, falls into sin, extraordinary efforts should be made by the church to bring him back into fellowship. In the next verses, 15 through 20, we find out what those extraordinary steps are.

First, the one who knows most about the sin of a fellow sheep (because it was against him or her) goes quickly and confronts, speaking the truth in love. If the other person refuses to listen, one or two others are brought along for the second meeting. Surely then the wandering sibling in Christ will listen and repent and return to the sheepfold, the church.

But if he or she refuses to listen to them, those who bear the authority of the keys of the kingdom of heaven, the shepherd overseers, must be told so that they will go and speak the truth in love. If the sinful person still refuses to listen, this shows that his or her heart is so hard as to be inconsistent with their profession of faith.

Thus the church leaders and members are to treat this person as though he or she is not a member of the church, not part of the sheepfold, but someone outside of the church. This is because his or her observable, outward words and actions deny the vows made to Christ and Christ's church. To use Ken Sande's terms, "This brother has moved from being an object of pastoral care to an object of evangelism."[2] Verses 18 through 20 show how this is a special form of evangelism, aimed at recovering one who has previously professed faith. It is only when sin continues that the full weight and authority of Christ, acting through the church, comes into play. This can be a powerful force to turn a Christian away from his sin.

Right after Matthew 18:15–20, Peter asks Jesus, "Lord, how many times shall I forgive my brother when he sins against me? Up to seven times?" (v. 21). This uneducated fisherman gets it! He realizes that what Jesus has been talking about is forgiveness, a rescue plan that leads to restoration and reconciliation. Where sin has built barriers, forgiveness tears them down! Then Jesus tells one of the most powerful parables recorded in Scripture, the parable of the unmerciful servant. God's forgiveness is unimaginably expansive! And because he has forgiven each of us so much, how much more should we be ready and willing to forgive those who have sinned against us? These two parables (the parable of the lost sheep—Matt. 18:12–14, and the parable of the unmerciful servant—Matt. 18:21–35) that express God's great love for his sheep serve as bookends to support the "book"—God's search-and-rescue plan found in verses 15–20.

A Mini Case Study

Confronting the sin of another is no easy task. It is one of the most difficult things we are called to do. Why is this so difficult? Fear of man, of course, but also fear of entanglement, so we tolerate even bad behavior. We live in a society that teaches each of us that tolerance is a great, if not the greatest, personal virtue. This is also true in the church. The world speaks much louder than the church these days and the values and lessons of that worldly mind-set flood the church.

We see a man treating his wife rudely even though both are members of the church. Yet no one confronts him about his bad behavior. We have been taught to keep our noses out of other people's business. If we try even to suggest such bad conduct is inconsistent with a Christian's character, calling, and life, we may be accused of judging. The peer pressure to ignore sin is tremendous. Our fear of man drives us to seek positions of compromise and then only surface solutions are reached without any real changes being made.

In church conflict this dynamic is in full force. One of the most cowardly acts of church leadership I (Dave) ever witnessed was the failure to confront an unrepentant pastor who had led his church into a yearlong divisive conflict. When they asked him to leave his position, he threatened legal action, so out of fear of retaliation church leaders provided a severance package equal to a full year of salary and benefits and a positive letter of recommendation to another church. With such a bribe he left quietly. There was never any accountability for his sin that had divided this body of wounded believers.

On the other hand, one of the bravest acts of leadership I was privileged to witness was by an elder board who had the courage to follow up on a fleeing pastor's sin by bringing formal charges to the ecclesiastical body holding his ministerial credentials. This meant hundreds of hours of gathering and preparing evidence and taking the time to testify before the church court convened to hear the matter in a distant city. It meant facing the former pastor's threats of civil litigation and withstanding the pressure from some denominational officials to merely let the matter drop. By persisting, however, those elders demonstrated that they loved the church, that they were concerned for the former pastor's eternal soul, and that they feared God more than any man.

They accepted the responsibility to be obedient to Scripture and "tell it to the church" (Matt. 18:17), so that through the Lord's process of meaningful accountability, the consequences of sin would be realized. Sadly, the process ended with the removal of the man's ministerial credentials because he never repented even in the face of clear evidence of his guilt. The church, however, was protected, the man was shown his sin and called to repentance, and Christ was honored as his process for discipline was faithfully followed (Matt. 18:15–20; 1 Cor. 5:1–5).

Apply This to Your Church Conflict

As you consider your church's present conflicts, do you see Christians who are being hypocritical? Do people profess faith in Christ and yet swim in the stormy waters of unrepented sin? Are you living this duplicitous lifestyle? The church is here to rescue you. The biblical process of loving confrontation and the involvement of others to help you come to your senses are God's design for eternal good in your life, now and forever.

Why does Jesus build his church around redemptive corrective discipline and speaking the truth in love? It is obvious, isn't it? It was our sin that put him on the cross. Can it be any less a process of our own accountability for sin that makes his church a true church, the spotless bride of Christ being prepared for her bridegroom? Kevin DeYoung and Ted Kluck write:

> It is no coincidence that the problems of the seven churches in Revelation 2 and 3 are followed by a majestic vision of him who sits on the throne (chap. 4) and the Lamb who was slain (chap. 5). The magnificent picture of the sovereign, holy God of the universe sitting on the throne and the Lamb at his right hand follows seven very practical, specific letters. Each of the churches is called to overcome. But how do they do that? The answer is found in chapters 4 and 5. There we get a breathtaking glimpse of God and the Lamb. Take your eyes off your earthly situation and gaze into heaven and see what true reality looks like. No matter the church's problem, what is most needful is to see God in his glory. The church may have lost her first love, may be persecuted or impure, may have bad theology and be spiritually dry, may be full of weakness and apathetic. Wherever the church is, the people need to know God better.[3]

Hopefully you are in a church that will speak truth in love when confrontation is necessary. We cannot change another person but the Lord can use us to help open the eyes of a Christian friend in need of change. We can do this by faithfully speaking truth in love. We are responsible for obedience and faithfulness. God is responsible for the results. "My brothers, if one of you should wander from the truth and someone should bring him back, remember this: Whoever turns a sinner from the error of his way will save him from death and cover over a multitude of sins" (James 5:19–20).

Questions for Reflection

1. Is it possible that conflicts have grown in your church because real relationships, deep, true fellowship in the Lord, have never developed? What could you do to encourage others in your circle of influence to move beyond the commonplace superficial friendships that characterize so many churches?
2. What do you fear most about confronting a fellow church member over his or her bad behavior? How do you think you could overcome that fear?
3. How would the conflicts confronting your church change if every church leader and church member began a "search and rescue" operation aimed at those caught up in the storm of conflict?

Recommended Resources for Further Study

Timothy S. Lane and Paul David Tripp, *Relationships: A Mess Worth Making* (Greensboro, NC: New Growth Press, 2008).

Alfred Poirier, *The Peacemaking Pastor* (Grand Rapids: Baker, 2006).

Ken Sande and Ted Kober, *Guiding People through Conflict* (Billings, MT: Peacemaker Ministries, 1998).

16

Forgive as Christ Forgives

Be kind and compassionate to one another, forgiving each other, just as in Christ God forgave you.

Ephesians 4:32

Instead of accepting premature compromise or allowing relationships to wither, we will actively pursue genuine peace and reconciliation—forgiving others as God, for Christ's sake, has forgiven us, and seeking just and mutually beneficial solutions to our differences.

The Peacemaker's Pledge

Although forgiveness is costly and can be painful, this is actually one of the most wonderful steps of redeeming church conflict. With our hearts fixed on worshiping God rightly, and having confessed our sins to one another, we ask, *How can I demonstrate God's forgiveness of me by forgiving others and helping them to do the same?* Belief in the gospel of Jesus Christ communicates powerfully your belief in personal forgiveness by God of all your sins. This new identity as a forgiven child of God now compels readiness and eagerness to forgive our fellow human beings. The overwhelming reality of God's eternal forgiveness of each of our personal sins should result in an overwhelming desire to forgive others their sins against us.

The Four Promises of Forgiveness

Peacemaker Ministries summarizes forgiveness with the following four promises:

- I will not dwell on this incident.
- I will not bring this incident up again and use it against you.
- I will not talk to others about this incident.
- I will not allow this incident to stand between us or hinder our personal relationship.[1]

As an individual in your church conflict, this means that whenever you forgive another person, you are committing to:

- Not replaying the incident or offense over and over again in your mind
- Not talking about the incident—to the other person or to others—unless it is necessary for further restoration of relationships or to promote and preserve the unity of the saints
- Working hard to appropriately address any material issues so that you can rebuild a relationship with the other person

Why should we go through all of this effort and hard work? Why should we forgive? Because God forgave us, and loved us, far more than we will ever be called on to forgive or love another person (Matt. 18:22–35). As Francis Schaeffer reminds us: "In the midst of the world, in the midst of our present dying culture, Jesus is giving a right to the world. Upon his authority he gives the world the right to judge whether you and I are born-again Christians on the basis of our observable love toward all Christians."[2]

Group Forgiveness

Usually it is most helpful to explicitly state the four promises to the person you are forgiving. But how do *groups of people* in a conflicted church forgive a person or another group of people? Chapter 4 discussed many of the dynamics involved in group conflicts and that groups aren't reconciled, people are. This means that, although we may be able to facilitate some level of group forgiveness, individuals may still need further help to forgive one another.

At the conclusion of many church conflict interventions, the church leaders (or one specific church leader) will often make some sort of confession to the congregation as a whole. It would be impractical for all five hundred or one thousand (or more) people in attendance at a church service or congregational meeting to respond individually to the confession with the four promises of forgiveness. So someone (frequently the lead mediator or another church leader from the denomination or convention) may invite those in the congregation who have forgiven the leader or leaders to so indicate by raising their hands or standing or some other similar sign. But further mediation assistance will always be offered to those people who are still struggling with bitterness or unforgiveness toward the confessing leader.

For example, in one church intervention case on which I (Dave) consulted, the senior pastor had come to recognize how he had failed by sinning against the congregation, specific church leaders, and specific church members. He wanted to make a heartfelt and detailed confession to the congregation but, as he prepared for his confession, he told the lead mediator that he was fully convinced that he was "putting the nail in the coffin of his ministry." He assumed that the church would require him to resign his pastorate because they would consider him worthless as a shepherd and a leader. So he preached what he assumed was his last sermon and made his confession.

The congregation responded: "You can't resign! You're not going anywhere. Now you have shown us the true heart of Christ. You have become the kind of pastor we have always wanted. We can learn from you. We will grow with you. *We forgive you.*"

The pastor's confession led to a totally opposite response from what he expected. The congregation was eager to forgive when he showed a true heart of repentance. And they did this in a most dramatic way. After his benediction, as the pastor was trying to sneak out the back door in disgrace, his church members literally grabbed him and forced him to come back into the building. A large group of people gathered around him and expressed their immediate and dramatic forgiveness of him.

Of course such rapid grace and forgiveness is not always the response. Even in this situation, a few people were so angry that they insisted on leaving the church. And no one on that intervention team ever promised the pastor that if he confessed, he would be forgiven or invited to stay. Sometimes the consequences of our actions are painful. Even after personal forgiveness is granted, church leaders sometimes still must resign their positions. But this example is just one of many reminders that you cannot script the Holy Spirit. And when God's children remember his lavish forgiveness, they will sometimes be filled with immediate grace to forgive others generously.

No matter what had happened, this pastor would have been okay. Co-laboring with Christ, he redeemed his church's conflict, and the sweetness of forgiveness was a beautiful testimony to the gospel.

Bitterness

Bitterness is common in church conflicts. Former friends stew in bitterness and fail to manifest any of the fruit of the Spirit listed in Galatians 5:22–23 (love, joy, peace, patience, kindness, goodness, faithfulness, gentleness, and self-control). Nancy Leigh DeMoss writes:

> The prevailing mind-set in our culture today (and far too often in the evangelical world as well) leaves us with permission to be coddled, even empowered, in our resentment, our broken relationships, and our unresolved conflicts. Sometimes well-meaning friends come alongside us, supporting our stubborn determination to exact payment from those who have sinned against us and sympathizing with our self-pity. But the Word of God is clear that the cost of unforgiveness is great. We cannot expect to live at peace with God or to experience his blessing in our lives if we refuse to forgive our debtors.[3]

DeMoss offers some of the best help we've seen to uncover bitterness.[4] The following statements can reveal a bitter spirit:

- I often replay in my mind the incident(s) that hurt me.
- When I think of a particular person or situation, I still feel angry.

- I try hard not to think about the person, event, or circumstance that caused me so much pain.
- I have a subtle, secret desire to see this person pay for what he or she did to me.
- Deep in my heart, I wouldn't mind if something bad happened to the person(s) who hurt me.
- I often find myself telling others how this person has hurt me.
- A lot of my conversations revolve around this situation.
- Whenever his or her name comes up, I am more likely to say something negative than something positive about him or her.

If any of these statements fit your present emotional state, you are probably bitter. Even if your bitterness feels temporarily good or justified, God is calling you to forgive, because bitterness is sin. As internalized anger, bitterness and resentment will bring you great harm—physically, emotionally, and spiritually.

I (Dave) witnessed a shocking example of this. A powerful businessman in the community and lay elder in the church refused to forgive a young and inexperienced pastor after the pastor had made a foolish decision and fully apologized for it. Initially, as I began the mediation, I thought it was a typical church intervention but soon realized it was the worst case of bitterness I have ever observed. This powerful man refused even to consider forgiving the pastor and demanded his resignation; rather than risk the loss of this man's financial donations to the church, denomination, and denominational seminary, the denominational leaders kowtowed to his demands and removed the pastor.

Throughout the mediation process—with much grandstanding on the part of this one church leader—many charges were raised about pastoral fitness and ability to lead. But at the heart of it all, this man was driven mostly by personal animosity toward the young pastor. By every word he said and his attitude throughout the process, in addition to his actions (including the demand that the pastor be removed), this man showed nothing but his hatred. It was actually a degree of hatred greater than I had seen in a lot of wartime situations. He would literally grind his teeth he was so bitter. As far as I know, he never forgave and no one in his church or denomination loved him enough to discipline him for his bitterness and hatred. It is a frightening thing to consider how he is going to have to answer to God for his heart, for the Bible says: "Do not take revenge, my friends, but leave room for God's wrath, for it is written: 'It is mine to avenge; I will repay,' says the Lord" (Rom. 12:19).

Mark Dever, as quoted by Josh Harris, has said, "If you do not live a life marked by love toward others, the Bible has no encouragement for you to think that you're a Christian. None."[5] We pray that you will show yourselves to be true disciples of Jesus by your love for one another (John 13:35) and your commitment to fleeing bitterness. In the words of pastor and theologian John Stott:

> Thank God there are those in the contemporary church who are determined at all costs to defend and uphold God's revealed truth. But sometimes they are conspicuously lacking in love. When they think they smell heresy, their nose begins to twitch, their muscles ripple, and the light of battle enters their eye. They seem to enjoy nothing more than a fight. Others make the opposite mistake. They are determined at all costs to maintain and exhibit brotherly love, but in order to do so are prepared even to sacrifice the central truths of revelation. Both these tendencies are unbalanced and unbiblical. Truth becomes hard if it is not softened by love; love becomes soft if it is not strengthened by truth. The apostle calls us to hold the two together, which should not be difficult for Spirit-filled believers, since the Holy Spirit is himself "the spirit of truth," and his first fruit is "love." There is no other route than this to a fully mature Christian unity.[6]

Disputable Matters

We can, at times, disagree with others and no sin is committed. Differences over personal preferences or mere opinions may not require confession and forgiveness. There can be many wise ways to view and respond to these situations. Although we might prefer for life to be black or white, in reality much of life is filled with the gray of disputable matters (see Rom. 14). A disputable matter involves an issue that is neither forbidden nor required in Scripture. To respond well to these somewhat confusing issues, we need to look to biblical principles to guide us, especially when no clear biblical precepts are present. Applying principles rather than being guided by direct and clear precepts in Scripture requires great wisdom, especially when differing perspectives can apply the same principle in the same situation in very different ways. Thus we should approach such things with great humility and "not go beyond what is written" (1 Cor. 4:6). According to Philippians 3:15, "All of us who are mature should take such a view of things. And if on some point you think differently, that too God will make clear to you."

Prayerfully, we strive to discern what issues are nonnegotiable and how identifying them can build unity of purpose. We sort out legitimate (biblical) interests from mere opinions, preferences, and human (worldly) desires. Then we apply biblical principles to dig out the most God-honoring and love-of-neighbor solutions. Contrary to personal preferences, the nonnegotiable will be consistent with the Lord's goals and desires for his church (propositional truth); and that which is wise will be clear, measurable, and subject to meaningful accountability.

> If the question we are attempting to answer is not disputable, then the answer will most likely be clear from Scripture. Otherwise, when our perspectives, preferences, convictions, and values lead us to diametrically different conclusions, we are called to pursue peace while we help others grow in their faith. We are not to insist that our position be followed if it causes another to go against their conscience. To persuade someone to take a course of action contrary to what they prefer is a far cry from persuading someone to take a course of action contrary to what they believe is right. Of course, in matters where our own conscience calls us to a particular position, we have been called to model humility, gentleness, and a willingness to learn and grow even as we stand on our convictions. . . .
>
> When different convictions exist on a given issue that falls into the category of disputable matters, in order to promote unity, it is best to begin by addressing the issues underlying each position with gentle and biblically informed counsel. In those instances where one person is unable to change his position, even though we have tried to find a mutually satisfying agreement and have sought biblical guidance, our freedom in Christ allows us to model Christlikeness by "giving up" our position in an attempt to "please [our] neighbor for his good" (Rom. 15:2). I am not being loving toward my spouse if I am

not willing to set aside my own positions in those "gray" areas not explicitly dealt with in Scripture. In the words of David Powlison, "Relationships have been destroyed when even minor preferences become life-ruling demands."[7]

Apply This to Your Church Conflict

Over and over again, the reality of Christian fellowship fails to measure up to the dream of conflict-free relationships and the truth that "love covers over a multitude of sins" (1 Peter 4:8). Jesus says that he gives us his peace (John 14:27) and we are one in the Spirit (Eph. 4:4–6). But all too often we are disillusioned, attacked, abandoned, hurt, worried, and afraid—*in the church*.

And yet God calls us to love. Consider John 13:34: "A new commandment I give you: Love one another." This is not calling us to love the people we enjoy, who are honorable and easy to love. This kind of love is pleasant and takes no effort or faith, no dying to self or suffering. But when Jesus calls us to show the world that we are his disciples by our love for one another, he is calling us to community that is markedly different from other groups. We are to have love for the undeserving—this is mercy. Our love must serve and set aside self-serving attraction and forgive those who fail us—just as God loves and forgives us even though we fail him. This kind of love reflects the Triune God to a watching world (John 17:20–23).

From an eternal perspective, we already *are* reconciled with and united to our brothers and sisters in Christ. Therefore, during any church conflict, we simply strive to become who and what we already are: *one in Christ*. We may differ over issues and hold conflicting positions on important questions, but those temporary things pale in comparison to our unity in Christ. Paul says: "As a prisoner for the Lord, then, I urge you to live a life worthy of the calling you have received. Be completely humble and gentle; be patient, bearing with one another in love. Make every effort to keep the unity of the Spirit through the bond of peace" (Eph. 4:1–3).

As we rely on God and remember how much we have been forgiven, we will be able to forgive others. God will give us the grace and resources to forgive. *Forgiveness* and *reconciliation* should be the hallmarks of our church. They are our testimony to a watching world that Jesus is our Lord. Part of the Great Commission is Jesus's promise to be "with you always, to the very end of the age" (Matt. 28:20). He who has initiated the church and made such a promise would not call us to forgive and then fail to give us all we need to obey him.

Thomas M'Crie wrote: "He will establish unity on the solid and immovable basis of immutable truth and eternal righteousness."[8] And we read in 2 Thessalonians 3:16, "Now may the Lord of peace himself give you peace at all times and in every way. The Lord be with all of you."

Questions for Reflection

1. What is the greatest evidence in your life that you have been forgiven of all your sins? If you are unsure, please read again the parable of the unmerciful servant in Matthew 18:23–35.
2. When should you forgive someone who has hurt you? Should their repentance and confession precede your forgiveness?
3. How have the discussions and stories of redemption in this book brought you renewed hope for the church?

Recommended Resources for Further Study

Chris Brauns, *Unpacking Forgiveness: Biblical Answers for Complex Questions and Deep Wounds* (Wheaton: Crossway, 2008).

Nancy Leigh DeMoss, *Choosing Forgiveness: Your Journey to Freedom* (Chicago: Moody, 2006).

Patrick H. Morison, *Forgive! As the Lord Forgave You* (Phillipsburg, NJ: P&R Publishing, 1987).

The End of Church Conflict Is Never the End

ACTS 15:36–41

If it is possible, as far as it depends on you, live at peace with everyone.

Romans 12:18

This life, therefore, is not righteousness but growth in righteousness, not health but healing, not being but becoming, not rest but exercise. We are not yet what we shall be but we are growing toward it. The process is not yet finished but it is going on. This is not the end but it is the road. All does not yet gleam in glory but all is being purified.

Martin Luther

As is true in all conflicted churches, *the end of conflict at Lakeview Community Church was not the end.* To this day some former members refuse to be reconciled. A small number of families still have the grief of estranged relationships. And as is true in all churches, sin and unbelief continue to tempt even believers, so we must remain vigilant in our battle—faith's fight against sin.

But thankfully, there is one part of LCC's story that is such a unique example of redeeming church conflict we shake our heads

217

in amazement to this day: *The members and leaders of LCC gave the church away!*

What does this mean? Exactly what we said, but, of course, since people are the church, we mean the church facility and property were given away. Once their *perspective* was fixed back on eternity; once they had *discerned* that their shared interest was actually to glorify God and fulfill the Great Commission; once all of the *leaders and followers* were *responding biblically* to the personal and material issues of the conflict, LCC realized that the best thing they could do to serve the "harvest field" of their community was to give the church facility away to a new multiethnic congregation that was meeting in the gym of a local high school, a group far better equipped to reach the local community as it was now racially and ethnically composed. That group was a Christian group of similar faith and belief and was, in fact, being led by a church planter who had graduated from the same seminary as the senior pastor. He even held his ordination credentials in the same conference that LCC belonged to!

Of course, at first the idea was to sell the property. Then the idea of giving the property away surfaced. This idea seemed far too radical. After all, the church property was worth well over three million dollars! But as they prayed together, the members of LCC became more than 90 percent united that giving the church's property away would be the best way to advance the kingdom of God and love their neighbors. And so they did. They invested in the kingdom by seeing these tools of the church as truly owned by God, which should be put to the best and highest use. Some of the congregation stayed in the new multiethnic congregation; others found new church homes closer to where they lived so they could serve more effectively. The lessons of church conflict at LCC had been learned.

Some may think this a sad end to the story. But remember again the definition of *redeeming church conflict*: intentional dependence on the humbling and heart-changing grace of Christ's Holy Spirit by turning relational crisis in the church into compassionate care as you take every thought and deed captive to him. This was God's result, not man's.

With joy and unity and God-centered, Christ-exalting *love* the members of LCC had done just what we mean by redeeming church conflict. They made an eternal investment in their community and the lives of those now living there. Co-laboring with Christ, LCC had redeemed their church's conflicts for God's glory and their spiritual growth.

—⸻—

As we near the end of the narrative of Acts 15, we find Paul and Barnabas working together in Antioch. Verse 35 says, "Paul and Barnabas remained in Antioch, where they and many others taught and preached the word of the Lord." Paul and Barnabas have returned from Jerusalem to the city where the conflict had erupted. They have delivered the letter from the apostles and elders. That conflict is over! Paul and Barnabas had been faithful partners as peacemakers. The truth of the gospel was preserved, error refuted, and the work of building the church resumed. The end of conflict is wonderful and beautiful.

But the end of one conflict does not mean the end of all conflict. Conflicts can erupt at any time. Immediately, in verses 36–39, we read of Paul and Barnabas falling into conflict that is so sharp they part company:

> Some time later Paul said to Barnabas, "Let us go back and visit the brothers in all the towns where we preached the word of the Lord. . . ." Barnabas wanted to take John, also called Mark . . . but Paul did not think it wise. . . . They had such a sharp disagreement that they parted company.

How can this be? Here we have two mature believers committed to the truth of God's eternal Word, leaders in the church who were preaching and teaching others what it means to be holy. Not only that, they have been peacemakers, bringing to an end a divisive conflict of major proportions. Didn't that experience teach them something about how to resolve disputes?

Here is the hard truth about conflict: as long as we remain alive the effects of sin remaining within us and the sin in the world will conspire to lead us into new conflicts. Theologians use the term "state of grace" to describe the condition we find ourselves in after our justification but before our glorification. Sometimes this state is described as "the already but not yet."

219

Paul and Barnabas's sharp disagreement and parting of company reflect the tension of living in the "already but not yet." Even if the substance of their conflict could fall into the category of opinion and/or preference rather than sin, the response to their difference of opinion could and should rightly be called sin because fellowship was broken and the fruit of anger was manifested.

In the church today we will face many similar situations. We will redeem one conflict just to see another arise. Of course, we should learn from our experiences and become seasoned veterans of conflict, knowing when and how to best apply the lessons learned from those previous engagements (opportunities). As commentator Matthew Henry notes concerning this personal conflict:

> We must own it was their infirmity, and is recorded for our admonition; not that we must make use of it to excuse our own intemperate heats and passions, or to rebate the edge of our sorrow and shame for them; we must not say "What if I was in a passion, were not Paul and Barnabas so?" No; but it must check our censures of others, and moderate them.[1]

Conflict is inevitable, as seen in the great conflict between Paul and Barnabas. No Christian can escape it and that is why we need to redeem conflict, not flee or ignore it. We include verses 36–41 primarily because it is in the text, and to ignore verses just because they include hard teachings or disappointing historical information is never a good principle of biblical interpretation. But we also do so to encourage you when future conflicts come to your church. *The "end" of church conflict is never the "end" of church conflict.* However, we remember, too, that our conflicts are never without hope. Paul and Barnabas eventually redeemed their conflict when Paul forgave Mark his immaturity by later praising him (see Col. 4:10; 2 Tim. 4:11; Philem. 24). There is always hope!

When the next conflict comes to your church, what will you do? There is only one response worthy of the title of Christian you bear: *redeem conflict for God's glory and for your sanctification and the sanctification of those you call your brothers and sisters in Christ.* Both Paul and Barnabas continued in ministry just as the church must do even when it faces conflict. The life of the church is as dynamic as the life of every person in it. Since we know change is the norm for each of us as we move through this life, so too is change the norm for every church. And with change comes conflict. The call to redeem our church conflicts will continue until the day the Lord returns and makes us perfect.

Even if your current "disaster" is averted or resolved, and even if there are beautiful testimonies of lavish forgiveness, creative solutions to material problems, and reconciled relationships, some people are still going to leave the church for reasons related to conflict. In the coming years, your members will struggle with sin and unbelief. Even with faithful discipleship and loving, gentle discipline, some members will be unrepentant, at least for a season. Sometimes even reconciled and loving Christians will need to part company graciously over debatable issues. Still, God calls us to faithfully redeem all of our church conflicts over and over again. This requires an eternal perspective that enables us to persevere through suffering, never returning evil for evil, blessing and never cursing (see Rom. 12:14), and trusting that God is sovereignly working all things together for your good and for his glory. The prophet Isaiah once called for such remembering:

> Do you not know? Have you not heard? The LORD is the everlasting God, the Creator of the ends of the earth. He will not grow tired or weary, and his understanding no one can fathom. He gives strength to the weary and increases the power of the weak. Even youths grow tired and weary, and young men stumble and fall; but those who hope in the LORD will renew their strength. They will soar on wings like eagles; they will run and not grow weary, they will walk and not be faint. (Isaiah 40:28–31)

The Illusion of a Conflict-Free Church

Many churches try to avoid dealing with their conflicts with the goal of keeping the peace or the illusion that things are as they should be. Here are some examples:

- A large church of more than three thousand members is going through a very difficult time. Several hundred members have fled. The pastor continues his long-planned and well-prepared sermon series unfazed, never using God's Word to address the conflict to provide guidance, bring comfort, add clarification, or discipline in the midst of the body's continuing meltdown. He acts as if his preaching schedule is inviolate. Rather than seeing God's present agenda for the church, he plows ahead on his schedule.

- Plans for an extravagant (and expensive) celebration service dominate church life as a new facility nears completion. These plans continue despite the fact that terrible conflict has split the congregation, litigation has been initiated, and financial support for the building fund has plummeted.

- Conflict has driven the senior pastor from his church. Within three weeks of his departure, the associate pastor is called to the position as the new senior pastor by a congregational vote, in spite of denominational policy prohibiting such an action. Lay leaders and church members ignore mounting evidence of the associate's contribution to the conflict and to the former pastor's departure.

- A church board conflict with the church's separate and independent school board has led to several of the most affluent and well-known church families leaving the church in protest. As supporters of the school, these disgruntled members do not see that they have any responsibility to the church and do not even consider the relevance of the promises made by taking church membership vows. In an attempt to isolate the conflict as a mere school issue, church leaders make little effort to confront and rescue these families. Membership vows are ignored and rendered meaningless.

Why are church conflicts like these ignored or actively denied when it is clear that things are not right at the church? Dr. Timothy Laniak of Gordon-Conwell Seminary reflects on the nature of such wilderness experiences this way:

Wilderness stories in the Pentateuch characterize God as the Guiding Shepherd. Israel's Divine Pastor led his people through the wilderness by pillars of cloud and fire. He made a pathway through the Red

Sea, and eventually led his people safely to their haven of rest (Ps. 77:19–20). Numbers appears to be a book about aimless wandering, but the summary in chapter thirty-three reveals God leading with a purpose. *Detours were a result of the community's unwillingness to follow God's direction and timing.*[2]

The "detours" that churches make into conflict frequently are the result of the "community's unwillingness to follow God's direction and timing"—to follow his agenda for that time and place. But when church leaders deny their call to be God's agents to redirect the church's path out of the detour, the rebellion is compounded.

If your church is embroiled in conflict, it should be embraced as God's new agenda for your church. Do not ignore it. Do not try to maintain a facade of a conflict-free church. Instead, embrace your conflict as an opportunity for individual and corporate spiritual growth. The preaching schedule, a celebration, the anxiety of a temporarily unfilled pulpit, or the ease of excusing pastoral oversight, as the above actual cases illustrate, are expendable fluff when compared to God's present agenda. Don't give in to "fear of man" idolatry. Don't be lazy. Turn away from your personal agendas and consider carefully what God is doing in the life of your church by asking the following questions:

- What does God want us to learn as we respond biblically to this situation?
- How can we ask the right questions about this conflict that will open opportunities for our people to stay engaged and not flee?
- From God's perspective, what are the things we should be doing next to resolve this situation? What needs to be done now, next week, next month?
- How do we demonstrate loving well in this conflict?
- Who else should be helping us as we strive to be sensitive to God's leading? Who will hold us accountable so we don't miss the lessons of this detour?

When church leaders embrace a conflict and recast it as God's agenda for growth, conflicts are usually shorter, less intense, and bear the fruit of positive spiritual growth.

A Mini Case Study

The conflicts at Cornerstone Bible Church (CBC) began to escalate when the leaders quickly elevated the youth pastor to the position of senior pastor after their former senior pastor resigned amid great turmoil. The younger man was popular with the congregation. He had done a good job with the youth and this was respected by both parents and older members of the church. But his transition did not go well. His preaching was uninspired and his leadership of the elder board confusing at best. But now the elders who had made the decision and urged congregational affirmation were finding themselves increasingly on the defensive as they attempted to justify their prior action. It seemed simply too difficult to admit error. It seemed too un-Christian to confront the failing pastor with his weaknesses. And the conflicts grew.

By the time we were engaged as consultants, several specific and visceral personal conflicts had ignited. Some were aimed at the pastor, some at individual elders. Things were getting ugly. It became quite evident to us that the pastor was ill-equipped to lead the church in times of peace let alone this time of conflict. After many hours of investigation and interviewing, we confronted the pastor gently with the reality of the fact that he was not, at present, qualified for the position he held. Reluctantly and fearfully he agreed.

Now came the hard part. How does he explain this to the elders who still support him? How does he go to the entire church to tell them they need a shepherd who can lead them as he has failed to do? And perhaps most painful, how does he tell his wife and two children that he needs to step down, to surrender his job and its financial security, and to seek an appropriate call elsewhere?

Of course some would be glad to see him go. They needed the help of God's Spirit to make this not about personality and feeling they had achieved a shallow victory. There were those on the other side who would feel humiliated that their efforts to "save the pastor" would be used against them as the pastor's own admission of failure would show that they had been wrong. Conflict and confusion ruled. Until . . .

At a late and long meeting with the elders, the mediation team confronted them with their responsibility to accept the burden of being peacemakers, not just peacekeepers. What were they to do? First, they had to look deep into the Scriptures and deep into their own hearts to realize that God wasn't working for their temporal happiness and joy. God was up to something more eternal—their holiness and his glory. This also meant that they were called to be faithfully obedient to his Word, regardless of the results that came to pass. The cost was potentially very high, both to the church and to each of them personally. But we're thankful that they listened to God, trusted his Word, and faithfully obeyed all that he required of them.

The following Sunday the leaders stood together before the congregation. The young pastor stood with them. The most widely respected of the elders spoke first. He said he felt respected by everyone but that was because he catered to everyone as a people pleaser, changing as conditions dictated, tickling ears for the sake of man's praise. He confessed to being two-faced and unworthy of the title elder, and he asked for forgiveness. Other elders spoke, each confessing how their own fear of man had drawn them to make easy decisions, to take the easy road as they led the church, the popular path that now stood them in the dark forest of conflict. They each asked for forgiveness.

Then the young pastor spoke. He admitted he took the senior pastor position out of pride and out of covetousness for the larger salary and the place of prominence in the pulpit. He wept. He acknowledged his sin. And he announced his resignation. There were some howls of protest. But most there that day realized something profound was happening and that it wasn't just about these men standing before them. Later some said they saw idols being slain and shepherds emerging from the ashes. Others admitted feeling small in the presence of men who had laid down their weapons of defensiveness and self-justification to pick up the gentle harmony of humility as they demonstrated a unity with the crucified Christ without concern for temporal consequences. This was a day that would be long remembered at CBC.

Several years have passed. I (Dave) have had contact with elders and members of that church from time to time. I've heard stories of those who left CBC to plant seeds of conflict in other neighboring churches. And I've heard stories of humility, people catching themselves as they were about to defend the desire (idol) of their heart and remembering the day that God put an end to all of that at CBC. But most of all I remember that young pastor who had decided that faking it in the church doesn't work. After some additional training, he joined a parachurch ministry dedicated to serving pastors who had been displaced by church conflicts. His testimony is that if we really listen we can still hear because God's process is still at work.

Is there hope to redeem church conflicts? Yes. Yes. A thousand times, yes! One day we may sit with God and all of his saints listening to the stories. In the interim, we are comforted in knowing that Jesus understands our suffering. He knows what it's like to be betrayed, attacked, and abandoned by his closest friends—by *Christians*. Jesus is with us in our church conflicts. He is sovereign over our church conflicts. We can pick up the cross of our conflicts and suffer well—God will give us the grace we need. *God gives us himself.* "Let us then approach the throne of grace with confidence, so that we may receive mercy and find grace to help us in our time of need" (Heb. 4:16).

Acknowledgments

This book would not exist were it not for three gospel-proclaiming ministries that exist to glorify God and serve the church: Peacemaker Ministries, The Christian Counseling and Educational Foundation, and Westminster Seminary California. Through their resources, training, and the professional relationships we enjoy with many of their leaders, we have both been equipped to serve Christians and churches in conflict.

At various times throughout this book, we have expressed and expounded on points that I (Dave) made previously in other articles on church conflict. Peacemaker Ministries has generously allowed us to use this content, as well as their foundational peacemaking principles, and for that we are extremely grateful.

As is always the case with a major writing project—and also with our service on Christian conciliation teams that intervene in conflicted churches—our families have sacrificed so that we could serve. How grateful we are to our spouses, Pat and Fred, and to my (Tara's) young daughters, Sophia and Ella, for bearing this load. We are particularly grateful to "Auntie" Dianne Kimm, Jennie Strong, and Michelle Moore for volunteering to babysit so that I could write.

And finally we are exceedingly grateful for the careful review that Professor Dennis Johnson lavished on our final manuscript. His book, *The Message of Acts in the History of Redemption*, is a must read for anyone studying the book of Acts, and his willingness to review our manuscript prior to publication was a tremendous gift to us. We are likewise grateful for the eagle-eye check that Laura Bikle gave to our almost-final manuscript. We thank our editor, Chad Allen, and the entire Baker Books team. And we are truly grateful for the proofreading generously provided to us by Amy Aldrich, Rev. Jason Barrie, Fred Barthel, David Bendor-Samuel, Lance Edling, Pat Edling, Chris Forrest, Allison Pickering, Rev. Robert D. Jones, Amy P. Laverman, Jonathan Parnell, Rev. Alfred Poirier, Keri Seavey, Rev. Robert Stuart, and Andrew Walker.

Appendix A

A Summary of the Acts 15 Model for Redeeming Church Conflicts

A Checklist for Christians and Their Churches

Perspective

In a church conflict, we can know for certain we have lost perspective if we begin to take matters as personal offenses. Conversely, if we see so-called opponents with eyes of compassion, we can know God is working in us to redeem this conflict for his glory and our growth.

❑ Maintain an eternal perspective (vv. 3–4); that is, set all conflict matters in the broader context of eternity so they remain appropriately viewed as temporary opportunities for spiritual growth.

❑ Remember that the gospel is at the core of the redemption of church conflict, and seek to glorify God in all you do (v. 11).

Discernment

In a church conflict, we can know we are on the path of healing discernment if we find ourselves spending more time listening than speaking. Further, as we carefully form and ask questions seeking group health rather than merely advancing a personal, favored solution, evidence emerges that God's work of redemption is advancing not only his interests but also our holiness.

❏ Don't contemplate final resolutions (quick answers to presenting problems) before a careful process of comprehensive problem identification has been completed and you have discerned the heart motivations and interests underlying various positions and issues (vv. 6–12).

❏ Identify every individual and group who must be considered in the conflict resolution process, remembering especially to look to God and his interests (vv. 12–21).

❏ Carefully identify apparent competing, underlying interests (motives) among and between individuals and groups (vv. 5, 8–11, 20).

Leadership

In a church conflict, if we embrace our personal and individual responsibility for leadership (and followership) within each of our own personal spheres of influence, we gradually become group problem solvers and increasingly turn away from mere narrow personal agendas. The more we see ourselves as shepherd-leaders (and faithful followers) serving others among God's flock, the greater the opportunity for creating an environment from which peace will flow.

❏ Being compelled solely by the love of Christ, remember your affirmative duty as a Christian to all other people involved, using biblical truth as your standard (vv. 8–11, 19–21).

❏ Demonstrate consistent servant-leadership and faithful biblical followership (vv. 7–11, 13–21, 31), remembering that it is for Christ you suffer and serve.

Biblical Response

One of the biggest mistakes people make in church conflict is failing to trust Scripture. In a church conflict, as we remember that Christ loves his church more than we ever will and that he has paid more for it than we ever will, our confidence in the Bible and our commitment to faithfully pursuing biblical responses to conflict will be clear and steadfast.

❑ Humbly confess your own contributions to the conflict (vv. 10, 19).

❑ Hold people and groups accountable for all sinful words and behaviors (v. 24) by practicing redemptive, corrective church discipline.

❑ Lavishly forgive one another in relational conflicts and apply biblical principles to discover God-glorifying solutions in substantive conflicts (vv. 13–20).

❑ Do a reality test on potential solutions by asking, Will this particular answer to this specific conflict lead to final resolution or generate more conflict? (vv. 19, 28).

❑ Implement decisions as wisdom dictates, remembering that true resolution will require clarity and finality (vv. 22–35).

Selecting an Outside Third-Party Church Conflict Consultant

The decision to call in an outside consultant to assist the church in working through its conflicts is one that should not be taken lightly. Until 75 percent or more of the official church leaders *and* 60 percent or more of church members can say they are no longer content with the state of the church (or state of the conflicts), calling in an outside consultant is premature and may create a new set of conflicts. That being said, waiting too long to call for outside assistance can also be an error, one made by many churches. The timing of the decision to call for outside help is critical and the right time is as soon as possible after the majority recognizes that something needs to be done.

Usually church leaders are the ones who initiate the process to call on the services of a professional, impartial consultant. Leaders should be unified to the greatest extent possible when this decision is made. However, in a conflict situation it is quite unlikely that unanimity will be reached. Differing factions among conflicted leaders should be appealed to on the basis of broad, transparent, and transcendent interests, such as, Do you believe that the divisions in our church grieve the Lord to the extent that he would urge us to get help? Or, What God-glorifying criteria do you believe would be needed before you could agree to employ a neutral third-party professional?

Scope of Professional Services

The professional being considered should provide a written proposal that includes, at a minimum, the following six components:

1. Background research
2. Education and training
3. Investigation
4. Conflict coaching and mediation
5. Reporting
6. Training and equipping for future conflicts

1. Background Research

First, the consultant being considered should ask the church for extensive background records: the past ten years of membership/ attendance and financial giving and spending records; all minutes of board meetings relevant to the conflict(s) and how these conflicts developed; any letters from members and regular attendees related to the conflict(s); the church's constitution, articles of incorporation, bylaws, and all policy manuals and governing handbooks (e.g., employee's handbook, new member's training manual, and so on); and any denominational Book of Church Order or Book of Discipline or other official publication of the church. A worthy professional will want to do as much background research as possible with these records before arriving on scene.

Just as the consultant must do work before visiting the site, so must the church leadership team. All official leaders (pastoral staff, elders, deacons, and others) and other key individuals in leadership roles (small group leaders, Sunday school teachers, staff support personnel, and others) must be committed to the biblical study of conflict resolution. A worthy professional consultant will require a program of self-study before the site visit.

2. Education and Training

The consultant's proposal should include at least two separate educational and/or training elements, one for leaders and one for all members and regular attendees. Leader training should include the role and responsibilities of shepherd-leaders, polity dynamics, group dynamics, the theology and practice of biblical church discipline, and the uniqueness of the church as a God-initiated yet human organization. Member training should address the theology of biblical peacemaking, how Christians are to resolve conflicts and be reconciled, the importance of membership vows, the importance of meaningful accountability in the church for the sake of individual and corporate holiness, and the call to follow biblically qualified and character-worthy leaders. Leaders should be required to attend teaching provided to members and attendees.

3. Investigation

The consultant should be able to completely explain what data gathering will be done through personal interviews with leaders, church members/regular attendees, and, as is appropriate, former staff, members, and regular attendees who left because of the conflict. The consultant should specify how data will be used, and copies of all data-gathering forms should be provided in advance to church leaders so they will be able to carefully evaluate whether the questions asked are appropriate to the situation. A proposed schedule for conducting personal interviews should be provided along with a description of the scope of the interviews and how gossip will be controlled and discouraged.

4. Conflict Coaching and Mediation

Group mediations are very difficult to effectively conduct, and the potential consultant should be able to explain how the dynamics of "stage performance," "fear of man," "mob mentality," and "control idolatry" will be confronted and managed. Usually individual mediations result in either reconciliation between those at the forefront of conflicts or clarity as to where irreconcilable differences exist. The consultant should be able to explain how either result will be used in the overall church conciliation process and when these results are best revealed to the congregation.

5. Reporting

Two types of reports should be discussed: verbal and written. Verbal reports to both leaders and members are important because they begin to satisfy expectations for feedback in a setting that will allow discussion and questions. This is also an important additional data-gathering opportunity for the consultant. These report times must be controlled by the consultant, however, to prevent further divisive words and actions. A final written report to leaders covering every aspect of the conciliation process, findings concerning the causes of the conflict(s), short- and long-term recommendations, and follow-up actions should be included. The purpose and recommended use of the written report should be explained.

6. Training and Equipping for Future Conflicts

The proposal from the potential consultant should describe how leaders and select members will be trained and equipped to deal with future church conflicts. The church will be making a significant investment of time and finances in the consultant and the process he or she will lead. As such, everything that can be learned during the process from the consultant will aid in the resolution of future conflicts through internal church resources.

Professional Qualifications

In addition to understanding the scope of professional services offered by a peacemaking consultant, church leaders should carefully examine his or her personal qualifications. An interview either in-person or by conference call is warranted. Usually a team approach will be proposed, and the qualifications of each potential team member should be examined. These qualifications include:

1. Theological education and experience in the church
2. Counseling training and experience
3. Mediation training and experience
4. Church conflict intervention experience
5. Leadership ability

1. Theological Education and Experience in the Church

The consultant leading the team should have theological education and significant experience with a wide variety of church governance structures and church traditions. Depending on the nature of the conflict(s), legal training and experience may be an important consideration to avoid actions that could result in litigation against the church. If legal expertise is needed, only a consultant with such training and experience should be considered.

2. Counseling Training and Experience

Depending on the nature of the conflict(s), it may also be important that the leader or a team member be a qualified counselor with training and experience to respond to the various counseling needs of leaders and members. Frequently personal issues of marriage, family, employment, and losses of various sorts must be addressed as elements contributing to the church's conflicts. Crisis counseling (addressing threats of suicide, violence, and so on) is often required, and the consultant's ability (education, experience, maturity, and confidence) to handle such situations should be considered. While the lead consultant and every team member may not be a qualified biblical counselor, every team member should have basic skills to recognize crisis situations, take appropriate intervention steps, and quickly engage other qualified people. The church has the responsibility to identify to the potential consultant any known persons of the church who may have issues that could be explosive so that contingency plans may be made by the team.

3. Mediation Training and Experience

Church conflicts are resolved as key individuals central to the conflict(s) are reconciled. This means the consultant must be an experienced mediator. Preferably, the lead consultant should be a Certified Christian Conciliator with the Institute for Christian Conciliation (a division of Peacemaker Ministries), with additional training in church conflict intervention. A mediator with the same or similar church tradition as the parties involved in the conflict may be helpful.

4. Church Conflict Intervention Experience

As this book has pointed out, church conflicts involving large groups of people are the most challenging environments for the work of reconciliation and peacemaking. The consultant attempting such work must have a thorough understanding of the many considerations and the many forces at play in such an environment. This is not a place for an amateur. Many churches desire to conduct a personal interview with the potential consultant to explore their convictions concerning various theological positions that may be part of the church's present conflicts. A professional consultant should be able to discuss intelligently such matters and assure church leaders that his or her personal convictions and/or bias will not influence the work.

5. Leadership Ability

The consultant must be a confident leader, able to face the strongest personalities of the church and not be intimidated. He or she should be a person with the presence to lead potentially divisive group meetings. The consultant should be a person worthy of everyone's trust and from whom all will take advice and counsel. There is a certain quality of self-assertiveness that the consultant must bear as a character trait that will also allow members of the church to accept his or her leadership. Of course the consultant must be a deeply committed Christian who brings evidence of his or her own deep need for the leadership of Christ.

Rules, Procedures, and Success Rate

Hiring a professional church conflict consultant is similar to engaging the services of an expert in any area. Thus the consultant's proposal should include specifications regarding the rules, procedures, and administrative aspects of the consultant's services. The scope of the consultant's work should be clearly set forth in writing (the Professional Consulting Agreement) before any work is commenced. This contract will include the date and length of the engagement, what the cost will be, when and how payments are to be made, and the specific rules that the church and consultant agree will govern the services to be performed.

Church leaders should ask how the potential consultant defines a successful outcome. At the end of our time serving on a conflicted church intervention team, we describe our efforts as successful if every person involved in the church conflict can say: "The Word of God was faithfully proclaimed. I am more confident in who God is and I see more clearly how he calls me to demonstrate my love for him by my obedience to him and my love for my fellow Christians. I recognize that no matter how personal this church conflict feels, it's not all about me. This is God's church and I have a role to play in contributing to the God-honoring resolution of these conflicts and the promotion of the unity of the saints."

Be wary if a consultant guarantees that every immediate problem in your conflicted church will be "fixed." There is rarely 100 percent harmony and unity among people associated with a church conflict. But within our definition of redeeming church conflict, every church member and leader can be successful in redeeming the church conflict because every church member and leader can be faithful.

Even within this definition of success, however, any consultant should also explain how he or she is going to help your church move toward a definitive resolution of the conflicts *inasmuch as it is possible*. The consultant should not merely offer a conflict management approach—that would only prolong the destructive influence of church conflicts. Rather, for the sake of Christ's reputation in the world, God calls on his people to do all they can to bring a definite end to conflict.

Ongoing Contact

You should have a clear understanding of how much ongoing contact you will be invited to have with the mediation team in the future. As professional mediators who have served conflicted churches, one of our greatest joys is hearing from former clients. Years after a church intervention, we will receive an email with an encouraging report of how the Lord is ministering to and through a specific church. A leader will reach out to us for advice on a new crisis or conflict. We hear great stories, such as grandchildren being born into a church that years ago seemed on the brink of closure, a new missionary venture being launched from a previously ingrown church, and the ministerial impact of a youth program initiated by an otherwise elderly congregation . . . and we rejoice.

God is great and glorious and he loves the church! So do we!

God bless you and grant you great wisdom as you prayerfully consider hiring a consultant to help your church with its current conflicts.

Notes

The Case Study That Still Shocks Us

1. The stories in this book are based on individuals the authors have met or known in real life, but specific details and personal characteristics have been altered or left out to honor privacy. Any resemblance to a specific real person the reader may know is purely coincidental. We did not each serve on all cases, and Tara did not serve on the specific case with the "shocking" ending.

2. The Slippery Slope is reprinted or adapted with permission of the publisher from Ken Sande, *The Peacemaker: A Biblical Guide to Resolving Personal Conflict,* 3rd ed. (Grand Rapids: Baker, 2004). © Peacemaker® Ministries (www.Peacemaker.net).

3. Dennis E. Johnson, *The Message of Acts in the History of Redemption* (Phillipsburg, NJ: P&R Publishing, 1997), 5.

An Important Theological Note

1. Johnson, *The Message of Acts,* 2.
2. Ibid., 5.
3. Ibid., 4–5.

Chapter 2 Seeking the Wisdom of Others—Is That Wise?

1. For example, the Presbyterian Church in America has an appendix in their *Book of Church Order* on biblical conflict resolution; the Lutheran Church Missouri Synod has *Ambassadors of Reconciliation* (www.hisaor.org); and the Southern Baptist Convention has *Winning the Real Battle at Church* (www.winningtherealbattle.com). Undoubtedly other churches and denominations have their own polity-specific resources as well.

2. Sande, *The Peacemaker,* 12–13.

3. Both Dave and Tara are members of Presbyterian Church in America churches and thus their convictions regarding theology and polity line up with the PCA (www.PCAnet.org).

4. Taken from the Peacemaker Ministries' *Peacemaking Church Resource Set* (Billings, MT: Peacemaker Ministries, 2004).

Chapter 3 Eternity Makes a Difference

1. Thabiti M. Anyabwile, *What Is a Healthy Church Member?* (Wheaton: Crossway, 2008), 27.
2. Timothy S. Lane and Paul David Tripp, *How People Change* (Greensboro, NC: New Growth Press, 2008), 7.

Chapter 4 Actions, Desires, and Beliefs

1. Ken Sande, *Managing Conflict in Your Church* (Billings, MT: Peacemaker Ministries, 1993), 9.

Chapter 5 Much Discussion and Debate

1. Sande, *The Peacemaker*, 249.

Chapter 8 Moving from Spiritual Blindness to Sight

1. Paul David Tripp, *Instruments in the Redeemer's Hands* (Phillipsburg, NJ: P&R Publishing, 2002), 279.
2. Ibid., 9, emphasis added.
3. Ibid., 285.
4. John Newton on spiritual blindness, "Excerpt from a Letter by John Newton," www.gospelweb.net:JohnNewton/newtononspiritualblindness.htm.

Chapter 9 Christian Duty within the Church

1. Wayne Mack, "Conflict Resolution in Marriage" (lecture series, 14th Annual NANC Conference, 1989). Available on audiotape from Sound Word Associates. Cited in Robert D. Jones, "Resolving Conflict Christ's Way," *Journal of Biblical Counseling* 19, no. 1 (Fall 2000): 14.

Chapter 10 Shepherd-Leadership

1. Descriptions are from Dr. Timothy Laniak, *While Shepherds Watch Their Flocks: Forty Daily Reflections on Biblical Leadership* (Matthew, NC: ShepherdLeader Publications, 2007).

Chapter 11 Biblical Followership

1. Laniak, *While Shepherds Watch Their Flocks*, 199.
2. We are quoting our mutual friend Amy Laverman, who uses this term frequently when she teaches on this topic.
3. Wayne A. Mack and David Swavely, *Life in the Father's House: A Member's Guide to the Local Church* (Phillipsburg, NJ: P&R Publishing, 2006), 81–82.
4. Anyabwile, *What Is a Healthy Church Member?* 100.
5. Ken Sande, *Love and Respect in Marriage* (Billings, MT: Peacemaker Ministries), as cited on www.Peacemaker.net.

Chapter 12 Accountability We Should Cherish

1. Edmund P. Clowney, *The Church* (Downers Grove, IL: InterVarsity, 1995), 269.
2. Ibid., 272.

3. Ibid., 90.

4. Ibid., 101.

5. Jonathan Leeman, *The Church and the Surprising Offense of God's Love* (Wheaton: Crossway, 2010), 17.

Section 4 Biblical Response

1. Ken Sande, *Guidelines for Christian Conciliation* (Billings, MT: Peacemaker Ministries, 2001), 17.

2. Sande, *The Peacemaker*, 12–13.

Chapter 13 How Can I Glorify God in This Mess?

1. Tripp, *Instruments in the Redeemer's Hands*, 284.

2. Barbara Miller Juliani, ed., *The Heart of a Servant Leader: Letters from Jack Miller* (Phillipsburg, NJ: P&R Publishing, 2004), 276.

3. This VBS curriculum was written by Pastor Jeff Hamling and is available for purchase at www.tarabarthel.com. The VBS incorporates principles from Corlette Sande's *The Young Peacemaker* (Wapwallopen, PA: Shepherd Press, 1997).

4. Alfred Poirier, *The Peacemaking Pastor* (Grand Rapids: Baker, 2006), 111.

Chapter 14 Owning My Contribution to Conflict

1. James Thompson, *Our Life Together* (Austin, TX: Sweet Publishing, 1977), 136.

2. David Powlison, *Seeing with New Eyes: Counseling and the Human Condition through the Lens of Scripture* (Phillipsburg, NJ: P&R Publishing, 2003), 132–40.

3. Sande, *The Peacemaker*, 126–34.

4. Ray Stedman, *Body Life* (Glendale, CA: Regal, 1972), 110–11.

Chapter 15 Speaking the Truth in Love

1. Mack and Swavely, *Life in the Father's House*, 188.

2. Sande, *Managing Conflict in Your Church*, 42.

3. Kevin DeYoung and Ted Kluck, *Why We're Not Emergent: By Two Guys Who Should Be* (Chicago: Moody, 2008), 252.

Chapter 16 Forgive as Christ Forgives

1. Sande, *The Peacemaker*, 209.

2. Francis A. Schaeffer, *The Mark of the Christian* (Downers Grove, IL: InterVarsity, 1970), 13.

3. See Nancy Leigh DeMoss, *Choosing Forgiveness: Your Journey to Freedom* (Chicago: Moody, 2006), 24–25.

4. Ibid., 58.

5. Joshua Harris, *Stop Dating the Church: Fall in Love with the Family of God* (Colorado Springs: Multnomah, 2004), 56.

6. John R. W. Stott, *The Message of Ephesians,* The Bible Speaks Today Series (Downers Grove, IL: InterVarsity, 1979), 172.

7. Tara Barthel and Judy Dabler, *Peacemaking Women: Biblical Hope for Resolving Conflict* (Grand Rapids: Baker, 2005), 189–91.

8. Thomas M'Crie, *The Unity of the Church* (Dallas: Presbyterian Heritage Publications, 1989), 64.

Conclusion The End of Church Conflict Is Never the End

1. Matthew Henry, *A Commentary on the Whole Bible* (Iowa Falls, IA: World Bible Publishers), 6:200.

2. Laniak, *While Shepherds Watch Their Flocks,* 190, emphasis added. See Numbers 13–14.

Scripture Index

Genesis

3:16 147, 148
9:16 56
45:8 149

Exodus

3:6 53
3:10–11 54
4:1 54
4:10 54
4:13 54
4:21 55
7:4 56
20:12 149

Deuteronomy

31:6 56

Joshua

1:5 52

1 Samuel

15:23 149

2 Samuel

23:5 56

Job

10:1 90
38:1–7 90

Psalms

23 57
23:4 135, 146
34 180
55:2, 4–5 24
57 52
77:19–20 223
90:4 58
90:12 58
118:8–9 34
119:28 38
139:23–24 108
141:5 196

Proverbs

3:5 34
3:11–12 155
3:34 194, 195
9:8 196
13:3 80
15:22 40
16:28 45
18:2 77
19:15 134
19:15, 19 180
19:27 97
20:5 88
28:11 71
28:26 34
29:25 52, 131

Isaiah

40:28–31 221
42:16–18 114
46:10 23
54:10 56
55:3 56
59:9–10 107

Jeremiah

17:5 34
17:7 34, 50
22:13 137

Ezekiel

34 202

Daniel

2:19–22 149

Amos

9:11–12 119, 173

Matthew

5:9 186
5:21–26 43
5:23–24 157, 176
5:24 53
5:43–45 190
6 110
7:5 185

245

Tara Klena Barthel formerly served as the Director of the Institute for Christian Conciliation, a division of Peacemaker Ministries. As such, she oversaw the delivery of all conciliation services and advanced conciliator training. Currently, she serves her family as a homemaker while regularly mediating, writing, and speaking at conferences and retreats. Baker Books published her first book in 2005: *Peacemaking Women—Biblical Hope for Resolving Conflict* and her first video series was released by Peacemaker Ministries in 2007: *The Peacemaking Church Women's Study—Living the Gospel in Relationships*. Prior to joining the staff of Peacemaker Ministries, Tara worked as an attorney and business consultant in Chicago. Tara, Fred, and their daughters are members of Rocky Mountain Community Church (PCA). To stay in touch with Tara online, please visit tarabarthel.com to friend her on Facebook (tara.barthel), follow her on Twitter (@tarabarthel), or participate in the redeeming churchconflicts.com blog.

Dave Edling left a law and business career to attend Westminster Seminary California. After eight years on the pastoral staff of a church in Southern California he joined Ken Sande at Peacemaker Ministries in Billings, Montana. He served at Peacemakers for ten years in various roles that included working with many churches facing conflicts. He has three masters degrees and a law degree and has frequently taught at seminaries and colleges across the United States. While now retired, he continues to volunteer in his church's ministry of biblical peacemaking and writes regularly for www.redeemingchurchconflicts.com, the website dedicated to helping churches think and practice in more redemptive ways about the opportunities presented by church conflict. He is also a retired Captain from the United States Coast Guard Reserve having served for over thirty years. Dave and his wife, Pat, live in Colorado Springs.

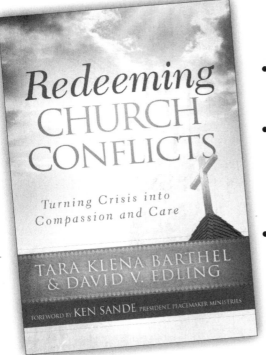

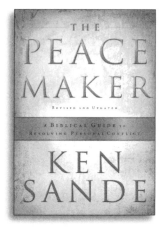

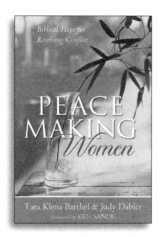
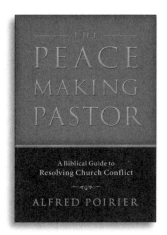